Praise for *You're the Boss*

"Sabina Nawaz expertly shares why business is personal and integrity is more important than authenticity for managers. You'll learn tactical tips to identify your own communication fault lines, trigger spots, and unmet needs as a manager. A must-read for all leaders!"

—Liz Fosslien and Mollie West Duffy, coauthors of the bestseller *No Hard Feelings: The Secret Power of Embracing Emotions at Work*

"Every leader ultimately faces defining moments—decisions made under the most demanding of circumstances that can make or break your career. Sabina's tools help you build your executive strength so you lead with intention, not reaction. *You're the Boss* will help you navigate high-stakes moments confidently, turn challenges into growth, and inspire your team—even when the heat is on."

—Robert J. Stevens, retired chairman, president, and CEO of Lockheed Martin

"Through her highly successful career as a manager, senior executive, and executive coach, author Sabina Nawaz has decoded the Micro Habits of effective managers. *You're the Boss* shares these hard-won insights with you, often using stories that range from hilarious to cringeworthy. If you're about to become a boss—and even if you've been the boss for years—and want to avoid preventable failures, this book is a must-read."

—Amy C. Edmondson, Novartis Professor of Leadership at the Harvard Business School and author of *Right Kind of Wrong: The Science of Failing Well*

"*You're the Boss* is like having a personal trainer for your career. Sabina's practical tools allow for deep self-examination while empowering you to make lasting change."

—Jim Guyette, former president and CEO of Rolls Royce, North America

"Sabina has a special ability to take abstract leadership challenges and theories and turn them into pragmatic, practical explanations and micro-suggestions. Highly recommended read for every manager and leader, full of actionable advice, behavior hacks, and tips."

—Amir Orad, CEO of Kraken

"Every manager owes it to their team to do the work to be a better boss so the team succeeds and thrives. This book is for all the managers who think they don't need a book on managing. They do. Sabina distills a library of management how-to books into one indispensable, insightful, and game-changing manual. Based on evidence and experience honed from decades of developing and coaching some of the top executives in the world, *You're the Boss* will make you better and surprise you—at any stage of your career."

—Kelly Jo MacArthur, former vice president
and associate general counsel of Amazon

"The wit, caring, and authenticity in Nawaz's writing make *You're the Boss* a comfort to read, not a boring, jargon-filled, executive-training-course syllabus requirement. Empathy brims through every page so the earnest reader doesn't feel like they're being lectured to or treated like an idiot or a failure. Reading the book, we learn that Nawaz has been there too! She knows exactly what the mixture of anger, confusion, elation, and depression feels like in that CEO or employee who's at their wit's end in the job. She affirms for us that we can get through whatever it is, if we take the time to reassess and apply her amazingly helpful techniques."

—Bisa Williams, senior fellow at the Yale Jackson School
of Global Affairs and retired U.S. ambassador

"Like most of you, I'm busy. I only read something I'm getting value from—page after page. *You're the Boss* passes that test easily. It zeros in on key management challenges and offers a wealth of practical tools and solutions. Of course, this doesn't surprise me. As CEO, I hired Sabina to run executive strategy retreats for my company, and I still follow her executive development approach to this day."

—Rodrigo Costa, chairman and CEO of REN, Portugal

"You're the Boss . . . is exceptional. It shares the same wisdom I experienced with Sabina firsthand as a CEO in great need of coaching on the pressure-cooker path to IPO. Her insights from decades of witnessing and guiding leaders are likely exactly what you need right now."

—Henry Albrecht, founder and former CEO of Limeade, and winner of the Ernst & Young Entrepreneur of the Year Award

"Sabina Nawaz delivers a powerful guide for leaders ready to unlock their full potential and navigate today's business complexities. I worked with Sabina early in my CEO journey, and her guidance was instrumental to overcoming challenges. This book is packed with real-life stories, actionable tips, and a touch of humor. Whether you're new to leadership or looking to sharpen your approach, Sabina offers proven techniques to lead from within, make an impact, and create a winning culture."

—Barak Eilam, CEO of NICE

"Sabina Nawaz is the real deal. After decades of understanding and coaching executives up to the absolute highest level, she has written some truly profound truths about ascending the ranks of leadership and the nuances therein. I wish I'd had this book at my disposal during my operating career, as it describes my experiences to a fine point. On your ambitious climb to the top, read this book to understand yourself, your peers, and your employees. What a gift she's given us all!"

—Blake Irving, board director and former CEO of GoDaddy

YOU'RE THE BOSS

Become the Manager You Want to Be
(and Others Need)

SABINA NAWAZ

SIMON & SCHUSTER

New York   Amsterdam/Antwerp   London
Toronto   Sydney   New Delhi

Simon & Schuster
1230 Avenue of the Americas
New York, NY 10020

First Simon & Schuster hardcover edition March 2025

SIMON & SCHUSTER and colophon are registered trademarks of Simon & Schuster, LLC

For information about special discounts for bulk purchases, please contact Simon & Schuster Special Sales at 1-866-506-1949 or business@simonandschuster.com.

The Simon & Schuster Speakers Bureau can bring authors to your live event. For more information or to book an event, contact the Simon & Schuster Speakers Bureau at 1-866-248-3049 or visit our website at www.simonspeakers.com.

Interior design by Carly Loman

Manufactured in the United States of America

10 9 8 7 6 5 4 3 2 1

Library of Congress Cataloging-in-Publication Data has been applied for.

ISBN 978-1-6680-2318-1
ISBN 978-1-6680-2320-4 (ebook)

The names and identifying information have been changed throughout this book to preserve anonymity.

For Matthew.
This book and so much of who I am and what I do
are only possible because of you.

Contents

Introduction

You're the boss.

You've made it to management (or at least are on your way there). Your smarts, grit, and talent propelled you to where you are. You know a lot. But what about what you *don't* know?

As an executive coach to successful bosses across the globe, I have spent more than two decades reverse engineering what makes someone an effective manager—and what can unwittingly take them out. The key comes down to one's willingness to unearth the hidden unknowns that, once excavated, generate success at world-class levels. Clients seek out my services because they want to be not just a boss in charge, but one who guides their team to generate excellent work and inspires everyone toward collective greatness. Isn't that what we all want as the boss?

While this book is based on the experiences of thousands of managers and executives I have coached, I also share insights from my own experience of becoming a boss at Microsoft, because my inquiry into what makes someone powerful as a manager started with me.

You see, I was a lousy manager, but I didn't start out that way.

A trained engineer, I was hired straight out of university by Microsoft and, within three years, worked my way up to my first managerial job as a test manager. Not long into that role, a few members of my team remarked that they thought I was the "best boss they'd ever had." What was I doing that made them feel that way? The answer was almost always some version of "Because you care."

I did care. I poured energy into coaching my team to be at the top of their game and genuinely cared about their well-being as humans. I openly supported their ambitions and encouraged them. In the world of tech, programming is generally considered far sexier than the testing we were doing, but several of the testers on my team came back to work with me after trying out programming, saying it was because of my investment in their careers and the collaborative energy of the team we had created. Don't get me wrong, I was tough with people as well. My boss labeled me "brass knuckles in a velvet glove."

After nearly nine years at Microsoft, I earned an eight-week sabbatical, during which I had an epiphany that changed the trajectory of my professional life. I realized that although I was close to being the only brown woman to become a corporate vice president at Microsoft at that time, *I didn't want it.* This led to a nontraditional move overseeing executive, leadership, and management development and succession planning for Microsoft, setting me on the path to becoming an independent executive coach. I brought my "best boss ever" skills with me to my new department, helping transform an overburdened team into a thriving one. I tuned in to what made each member of my team feel most engaged. Working in collaboration, we rearranged their responsibilities so they did work that fulfilled rather than drained them, which in turn yielded kick-ass results. Together we posted a 400 percent hike in productivity without increasing headcount or budget.

Then everything changed.

Shortly before my first son was born, my boss announced she was leaving the company. I said I'd think about stepping into her role when I returned from parental leave, and she replied, "No, no, it's not an option; you are already slated to take over my job. *Tomorrow.*" Overnight I went from being responsible for management development to overseeing the professional development of the entire company—all ninety thousand employees.

The morning I was slated to fully return to work from parental leave, my assistant called. "Where are you? There's a meeting with Steve in half an hour." I knew nothing about that meeting or what it was about, except that it was with Steve Ballmer, who was CEO of the company at the time. I hurriedly slashed on some lipstick and raced out the door while asking my assistant to scroll through communications to get me up to speed in time for me to walk in. That should give you some idea of the pace and demand that greeted me, set against the backdrop of the utter exhaustion of having a newborn at home.

Without realizing it, I slid from being a caring and supportive boss to one who was snippy and belligerent. Under crushing deadlines, I had no time to explain anything in detail. I didn't have the patience to nurture people in their career development; I figured, *They're adults, they'll figure it out.* Ditto for worrying about how my actions as a boss were impacting my team and their well-being. This was business, not personal. At least that's what I told myself.

In my rush for efficiency, I lost connection. When people came to talk to me, I would leave my fingers on the keyboard to silently convey they were taking up valuable time. On my drive home one night, I decided to maximize my time and called one of my direct reports to conduct her performance review. She was shocked I was doing this while driving, signaling that she wasn't important enough for me to sit down with her and have a conversation face-to-face. On another occasion, one of my assistants, Anne Marie, came into my office and said, "I totally understand if you say no, but someone approached me from another department for a project manager job. I know I've only been here for three months, but may I interview for it?" My immediate answer: "No." Not *What is the timeline for this opportunity?* or *How important is it to you?* Just an abrupt "No."

I also lost the plot when it came to distinguishing between managing and micromanaging. Case in point: we ran an exclusive three-day event with Bill Gates and Steve Ballmer, attended by high-potential employees about three positions down from them on the organization chart. Steve was concerned that we might have left the umlaut off the name of an attendee. Rather than trusting that my number two, Janice, who was always fastidious with details, had thoroughly fact-checked the list, I steamrolled over her assurances and demanded that she recheck on the spot the spelling of all fifty attendees' names. When one (literally one) of the highly coveted swag pens given to each participant didn't work, I was so irritated that I made Janice and another person on my team come in each morning at dawn before the day's program started to test all fifty pens for future events. I had no clue that the umlaut and pen stories were roiling through the hallways of my department and beyond like a vicious fireball, spitting off more and more sparks with every retelling. I had become the böss from hell.

I had no idea until my colleague Joe came to see me in my office. Under normal circumstances, I would have been happy to see Joe, because he always challenged me in intriguing ways about management development, but all I could think when he walked in was *No time . . . no time!*

In his tactful way, Joe sat across from me and said gently, "I think you may not be aware how you're coming across and how it's affecting your team."

Ridiculous, I thought, frankly irritated. I had a long history of being an excellent boss. I'd know if I was making missteps. Yes, okay, maybe I was a little less warm and fuzzy than I'd been in my former position, but I had a far bigger role now, in which I needed to prove myself.

"You're making people like Anne Marie cry with your comments."

At that, I quickly took my hands off the keyboard and gave him my full attention. I'd taken Anne Marie's assurance that she'd understand if I said no at face value and completely missed the opportunity to be not just the boss in charge, but also the one helping manage the skills and needs of my team. Hearing that my people were feeling dismissed, judged, attacked, and afraid of screwing up because of me was a bucket of ice water in my face.

That was a turning point for me.

Besides cleaning up my act as a manager, I used my engineer training to dissect and reconstruct what it means to be genuinely successful in a role of authority. How had I veered so far off course? What makes one manager become a superstar and another crash and burn? How do well-meaning bosses end up making their teams miserable? Worse, how does all that happen *without them knowing it*? I started hunting around to understand how power shields us from seeing our missteps while the increased pressure of high-level roles affects our ability to self-regulate our behavior.

I arrived at the conclusion that there are rarely "bad" bosses, only good people with the best of intentions who unwittingly cross the fine line between good intentions and bad behaviors. And they are everywhere (including in the mirror). I came to understand a simple truth that eventually became the basis of my life's calling as an executive coach: as our job description expands, we must mindfully navigate the combined forces of greater pressure and power—*or else pressure will corrupt our actions and power will blind us to the impact of those actions.*

The best of the best seek my coaching because they know the key to being the best is always striving to be better, to uncover what you *don't* know. In our work together my clients learn to navigate the perils of pressure and power without having to overhaul their personalities or develop traits they don't already possess. This book is a collection of the insights and strategies that have allowed them—and now you—to upgrade their skill set to meet their elevated level.

Throughout this book I'll share many of the insights and results of data I've uncovered that have transformed the careers of thousands of managers. The backbone of this book is more than twelve thousand pages of data I have amassed through my research, coaching, and thousands of interviews. These interviews are done as part of what's called a "360 review," in which I interview twelve to fifteen of my clients' colleagues to gather detailed feedback about them. From that feedback, I assess themes that emerge of their managerial style, both positive and corrective, so my clients can see the unvarnished truth of how they are performing as a boss. Often, they are quite surprised by what they learn, some even shocked. As you'll discover in stories shared throughout this book, many find out the very behaviors they believe are germane to their success are in fact thwarting their efforts. With these raw truths in hand, we then work to apply strategies to successfully navigate the increased power and pressure of their role so they can inspire excellence and fulfillment rather than conflict and frustration.

With over two decades of experience identifying the most common themes across 360 reviews, I developed the system in this book that pinpoints exactly where and when we can most easily fall off track and strategies to course correct that have been time-tested in the hallways and virtual meeting rooms of thousands of executives.

This system will enable you to:

- Understand the critical truths and common misperceptions about power
- Identify where and how your communication breaks down in ways that hinder your effectiveness
- Avoid the common costly mistakes generated by unmanaged pressure
- Apply practical, field-tested frameworks for leading with greater impact and efficacy
- Prevent and neutralize friction in your interactions and help your team navigate conflict more cohesively

Part One reveals the surprising and often unseen ways the terrain changes as we get promoted, and shows the nuanced shifts necessary to thrive at this next level. Part Two debunks the common myths about being a boss that can (and often do) generate career-sabotaging mistakes when left unexplored. Part Three delves into what I call Power

Gaps—chasms that can open between you and those who work for you that unwittingly blind you to the impact of your behaviors. Part Four identifies what I refer to as the Pressure Pitfalls, which are the hidden pockets of self-sabotage we can fall into when pressure goes unmanaged. But it's not all doom and gloom! The information you'll discover will instantaneously shift your thinking and show you clearly what you need to lead with the efficacy and impact you desire. Throughout, you'll find diagnostics to help you assess where you stand and tools to get you to where you want to be.

Whether you're a new manager or have been in the C-suite for years, this book is a guide to empower you with a wealth of tactics and strategies essential for thriving in every stage of your career. By unearthing and meeting all the unknown forces head-on, you will have the clarity and confidence at your disposal to show up in every interaction as a world-class boss.

PART ONE

THE (SURPRISING) VIEW FROM THE TOP

CHAPTER ONE

New Level, New Rules

The very first thing I did upon landing in America was throw up.

I was twenty years old and headed for my junior year as a transfer student at Smith College. As one of the seven fortunate students from the Modern High School for Girls in Kolkata to have been offered a scholarship, there was no way I was going to let the fact that I'd never been on an airplane deter me. Besides, I love an adventure.

After bidding a teary farewell to my family at the airport, I had flown to London for a one-day layover. I stayed with a cousin who made me a lovely but rich breakfast in the morning and sent me off with some special chocolates, which was a big deal for me. I'd never seen this kind of abundance. The chocolates were so good that I ate tons of them on the flight from London to Boston, washed down with about a quart of sweet orange juice, which I'd also never tried. Just as the pilot announced, "Welcome to Logan Airport," I was heaving the overindulgence into the airsick bag.

At the airport in Boston, I looked around for water to rinse my mouth. I asked someone where I could find some and they pointed me to a water fountain. I had no idea what this hanging stainless steel contraption was. Back home, we'd get water from a tube well, boil it, and put it into an earthenware container with netting on the top to keep the flies out.

Later that day, I went for a walk to mail the letter I'd written to my family on a cocktail napkin during the flight. But I couldn't seem to find a mailbox. What I thought was a mailbox was actually a fire hydrant; mailboxes in India are red. Why was this mailbox so low to the ground? Where was the opening? This was just the beginning of my stranger-in-a-strange-land experiences. It took me the better part of the semester to get comfortable with these unfamiliar American ways.

I share this story as an allegory for how disorienting it can be to step into a new terrain. Everything from the level of demands and eyes on you to the volume of high-impact decisions you need to make to how your team behaves around you shifts the instant you step onto the big stage—and that can be more than a little unsettling.

Take Michael, for instance. I first met Michael when he was on the rise at a sports management firm. Fast-talking and confident, with charisma for miles, he was one of the youngest people promoted to senior agent in his company's forty-year history. As an attendee of one of my two-day workshops, Michael shared with the group how he had fantasized about being the boss for a while. He had a lot of ideas and just as many critiques of his current supervisor: *If only I were in charge, here's how much better things would run . . . How hard can that be? Why isn't my boss setting the right direction? Doesn't he see where we're lacking? Why isn't he thinking about ways to make us the best in the business, like I am?*

The next time I heard from Michael was a year later, a week after he was appointed managing director of his East Coast office. Ever the quick wit, the subject of his email read, "Made it. Now what?"

In our first coaching session, Michael admitted with uncharacteristic humility that he was surprised to learn about a whole layer of issues his prior boss had been managing to which he had never had exposure. The responsibilities that now fell upon him were more copious and intense than he'd imagined. He was prepared to oversee the budget, address underperforming employees, and make sometimes challenging hiring decisions. What he did not expect was for the heads of satellite offices to start jockeying for resources immediately or for political fissures to open that he had no idea existed, encouraging everyone to vie for his alliance. Every day, he had to make tough calls on decisions large and small that could set his firm on an upward trajectory or cost them important clients. He was more than a little rocked by the volume of meetings and people who needed his input to move forward.

"But here's the weirdest part," Michael said. "All of a sudden, the people I've worked with for years are treating me differently. One guy I came up the ranks with calls me 'Boss' in a way that sounds like he's joking, but I can tell he isn't. It feels as if no one is real with me anymore. Even my jokes are mysteriously funnier, if you know what I mean?"

I assured Michael I knew exactly what he meant. Maybe you do, too?

I work with top-level executives from a wide range of organizations who find themselves in similar situations. Power can feel very different than we expected it to. After the celebratory bubbles settle, like many other managers, you may find a strange emptiness creeping in as you realize that being in charge isn't all fizz and fantasy. The stakes have changed along with the power dynamics. Overnight, you go from being one of many voices in a room to *the* voice of authority. Decisions carry a lot more weight when the ultimate call stops with you. As Michael experienced, your team may treat you with a mix of deference and distance, which feels more isolating than validating. Peers who were once trusted pals might now take little jabs at you or box you out, shrouding their passive resentments and annoyances with fist bumps and treacly praise. A lot of my clients lament the days when problem-solving meant driving concrete outcomes, not a garbage can overflowing with others' Kleenex or an inbox jammed with roadblocks and complaints. Even if you celebrated your ascent long ago, you may lie awake in the wee hours of the night wondering when everyone will find out you don't really know what you're doing, or if you even want this responsibility of authority.

Being the boss sounds thrilling, and in many ways, it is. Autonomy, a sexy title, more money and prestige, shiny perks—that's the fun stuff! You've worked hard and deserve to reap the rewards. You get to jettison some of the menial tasks of your previous role and sink your teeth into meaty challenges. You're finally given the autonomy to implement your vision and make a real impact. Everything you've worked for is coming to fruition as you step up into a power role, and that can—and should—feel like a big win.

At the same time, the title is just the anointing. The question, as Michael's email posed, is what do you do once you get there?

It would be easy to assume that being a high-performing professional means you'll be a highly effective boss. Yet as executive coach Marshall Goldsmith reveals in his book *What Got You Here Won't Get You There*, the skills it takes to get to the top are not the same as the ones you need to keep you there. What you do and *don't* do, what you say and how you say it, how you think and respond to the rise in power and pressure all require leveling up. To succeed and thrive in a role of authority demands a full-scale recalibration to that higher level. That starts by seeing with full clarity what changes and how you need to shift accordingly when you ascend to the role of boss.

Redefining Success

How do you define success?

For most ambitious individuals on their way up, success means generating excellent work and garnering the attention and rewards for it. While we ideally strove to collaborate and be someone our peers ultimately wanted to work for (a proven marker of a successful boss), our focus was naturally and rightly on *our* work, *our* path, *our* ascension. Success meant us personally kicking ass on our individual career path. That drive to stand out is not selfish, but understandable as we compete to be the winner who will get promoted.

Yet success as a boss is a very different animal.

As I tell many of my clients, it's no longer all about you, sunshine. When you become the manager of a team, your success now derives from *their* success. The goal is not to burnish *your* brilliance but to empower *them* to feel brilliant. Showcasing your output may be what got you where you are, but now you need to rewire who gets showcased and what "output" means. Recalibrating to focus on driving your team's success is the critical distinction between being a standout employee and a standout boss.

Before, your mission was to generate the work. Now, however, your mission is to create and hold the container for others to generate their best work. By "container," I mean the larger goal, the desired outcome, the nonnegotiables as well as sufficient psychological safety. As the powerful force operating behind the scenes, you accelerate and activate the work of others. For instance, before becoming the boss, you may have had to create the slide deck for a client presentation. Now your job is to give your team clear guidance on the objective and parameters for that slide deck so they can do the hands-on work to meet that goal. That's what strategic thinking means. It means being able to step back, see the bigger picture, and drive the entire mission and team toward the greater desired outcome. Rather than manage every detail and issue as you once did, you empower *them* to manage those details and issues. Your job is no longer to work solo with laser-focused determination to ascend but to set the North Star to empower your team to rise along with you.

Sharing the limelight benefits you as well as your team. An extensive study done by Yuan Zou and Ethan Rouen at Harvard Business School showed that managers who elevate others experience greater rates of employee retention and are twice as likely to rise to the ranks of CEO. Having said that, shifting from being the star player to the coach can be challenging, as we are hardwired to protect our relevance and avoid our own corporate mortality. Many of us think it's a zero-sum game:

if they shine, I'll be dulled by comparison. There's an inherent scarcity built into the ascension mindset, as there can be only *one* best.

Take Armond, for instance. As the managing director of a design team at a toy manufacturer, he was asked to give a report to the CEO summarizing what each of his direct reports had accomplished or issues they'd dealt with that past week. His 360 revealed a habit of positioning innovations from his team as his own, both subtly and overtly. When I presented that information to Armond, he offered up a common justification: "If I'm just the person who passes along the information and approves paperwork, what's my contribution here?"

Armond poses a good question. If we allow our team to shine, how do we stand out? If we delegate, what's our value? How do we stay relevant at the top while empowering those who work for us?

The answer is to shift from a scarcity mindset to one of abundance.

To understand and cultivate an abundance mindset, we first need to get our heads around what scarcity looks and feels like. Scarcity isn't always about money. Scarcity in our professional lives is a fear of not enough to go around: not enough opportunities, recognition, connections, or rewards. Scarcity is grabbing all the goodies and guarding our treasures—from our contacts to our knowledge and ideas—to keep our singular edge.

Scarcity is competing. Abundance, on the other hand, is collaborating. An abundance mindset means soliciting ideas and input from your team, freely offering up positive feedback, coaching your team to be their best, and sharing your ideas, your contacts, your expertise, and yes, the limelight. A scarcity mentality clings to an "it's me or them" dynamic, whereas an abundance one makes room for others to ascend along with you. The truth is that there is far more space at the top than you think.

For five years, I worked with Bill Gates and Steve Balmer on Microsoft's succession planning. Each year, we would spend two weeks holed up in a conference room meeting with all the presidents to discuss who in their divisions was in line to succeed them. Year after year, nothing excited the executives at the top levels more than when they found talented people who could be nurtured and brought up to the highest positions in the future.

Having worked with many executives since that time, I see this as a universal dynamic. The bar to succeed at the top is high, and many don't make the cut—or, even if they did or could, they weed themselves out because of the pressure. My clients at the highest levels are *desperate* to find people they can mentor and help cultivate the skills and fortitude to climb up. Secure in their own value, they break out the proverbial bubbly anytime they spot someone who shows a glimmer of being able to succeed them one day.

The takeaway for you as a manager is that you can and should continue to be the best in your role—you just don't have to be the *only* best. You don't have to outdo your team. Each team member has their own role. In an abundance mindset, there's plenty of space in the talent pool to invite those who work for you to join you.

How exactly do we cultivate an abundance mindset? By practicing generosity and modeling it from the top down. Despite the inherent competition baked into getting ahead, plenty of research proves that generosity pays off exponentially. Wharton professor of management and best-selling author Adam Grant published evidence in a 2013 McKinsey report illustrating a direct correlation between employees helping one another and increased sales revenues, creativity, productivity, and performance quality in a variety of industries. In interviews with approximately eight hundred managers working in Sydney and Silicon Valley, a team from the Macquarie Business School in Sydney, Australia, found that company cultures in which information and resources were shared openly had a distinct competitive advantage in terms of innovation, efficiency, and quality.

As you explore the insights and tools throughout this book, you'll discover many opportunities to expand your definition of success. You'll be amazed by how much your status and success rise as your team rises. You shine because they shine. You ascend because they ascend.

This is the abundance mindset at work.

Coaching Consideration: Do You Need to Get Over Yourself?

My client Jaclyn emerged from our work together proud of the way both she and, by extension, those who worked for her had leveled up. After a year of internal skirmishes and bitter complaints making their way to Jaclyn's boss, her team was collaborating and performing significantly better. One guy who initially had stinging commentary about her tendency to hoard the spotlight was now a total convert. I asked Jaclyn what she thought was the most powerful shift she had made, and she replied, "I learned to get over myself."

To cultivate an abundance mindset, might you possibly need to do the same?

Understanding Hidden Power Dynamics

On a rare quiet Friday afternoon, Liza went on a coffee run with Zoran, one of her top people. As CFO of a start-up, Liza's days were usually jammed from the minute she checked her email on the treadmill at 6 a.m. until she finished her last call on the drive home in the post-dinner hours, so it was a treat for her to get a hit of fresh air and a chance to chat informally with a member of her team whose company she enjoyed. As a moving truck passed by them, Liza mused aloud whether their start-up would move when their lease was up in two years. Within days, the hallways were abuzz with people campaigning for choice office space, flooding Liza's inbox and ears with ideas of the ideal location for the new office—next to each person's hometown, naturally.

As Liza discovered, when you're the boss, there's really no such thing as "off the record" anymore. Being in charge comes with a sticky web of interpersonal power dynamics that underpin almost everything you say, do, and generate (or don't generate) as a manager. It's easy and frankly convenient to brush over this by-product of authority, but your success hinges on your ability to understand and navigate the dynamics that arise when hierarchy enters the equation.

Our complex relationship to authority starts from the time we are infants. When the adults in our lives use their authority well, they nurture us, teach us, guide us. Other authority figures unfortunately can also abuse their status or use it capriciously. If you start to layer in your personal history and the cultural legacy you carry around the concept of authority—say you have brown skin or were a liberal-minded teen growing up in a traditionally conservative family—that complicates matters even further. Every time we are in a relationship to authority, it activates all those historical relationships. Each one of us comes to our interactions with authority toting these layers of packed baggage.

The human drive to please authority figures traces back to evolutionary behaviors. If your alpha parent didn't like you, you were dead, period. No food, no shelter, no community, no survival. Good luck out there in the wild on your own, kiddo. We are hardwired to want to please those guardians of our fate. Fast-forward to modern times, and that guardian is you. As the boss, you are in control of the destiny and livelihood of the people on your team. As Ronald Heifetz and Marty Linsky write about in their excellent work on adaptive leadership, employees look to their boss for three things: protection, order, and direction. Your role as the provider of that protection, order, and direction makes you the alpha by default.

Thus, whether you register this consciously or not, every sigh, bored look, or rushed exchange you have is hyper-scrutinized, analyzed, and interpreted (usually as negative) by those who work for you. If you doubt it, think about how tuned in you are or have been to the body language and moods of your own bosses. My research bears this out to an astonishing degree. Almost every single direct report I've interviewed is convinced their manager's mundane actions were targeted toward them. As the boss, if you frown as you walk down the hall, they think you are frowning at them. Something as minor as firing off a quick, vague email on a Sunday asking a direct report to stop by your office tomorrow can kill their weekend as they try to decode your true intentions and wonder if they'll have a job come Monday. An unintentional grimace from a blister on your pinky toe during an employee's presentation can send them reaching for the Tums in their bottom desk drawer. As we'll discuss more in Part Four when we unpack the proven business ramifications of triggering your team members' biological fight-or-flight responses, these unintentional upsets hurt far more than just your employees' morale or digestion.

Another complex power dynamic stems from the fear of speaking truth to power. That's a risk few are comfortable taking. Thus, as the boss, you might notice that people on your team tend to agree with you . . . a lot. Not only are your jokes mysteriously funnier, as Michael noted, but your ideas are more brilliant and advice more salient. While I'd love to tell you that's because you're a prophet of corporate wisdom, much of the concurrence is a by-product of your elevated status. Validation may feel satisfying to your ego, but your effectiveness takes a hit when those who work for you obscure bad news or critical opinions that could vastly improve your impact.

One of the first retreats I ran for a CEO I work with was for his team in a southern European country. In that country, events tend to be a little loose timewise. Few things start at the appointed hour, and the schedule stretches based on how long the smoke break is; the hotel staff where we held the retreat told me they were used to constantly reheating food to keep up with the changes in timing. I told Luis, the CEO, that I planned to run the event on a tight schedule and needed his help to stick to the timeline. After the first day, the hotel manager sought me out to say the delighted staff had never seen an event run clockwork like this.

On the second morning, Luis was not in the conference room five minutes before we were set to start. I asked Maria Theresa, the head of HR, where he was, and she told me he was still in the breakfast room.

"Okay," I answered. "I'll go get him."

Dead silence and a deer-in-the-headlights stare from Maria Theresa followed. After a beat, she snapped to and replied, "Yes, yes . . . good. You're the only one who can do that."

I was so surprised. We had an agreement to be timely, Luis was running late, so it seemed pretty straightforward to remind him of our imminent start. What was so scary about it?

Later that morning, when Luis stood to speak and heard a bit of noisy construction outside the windows, he said to no one in particular, "I'm loud enough, aren't I? Do I need a microphone?"

There were muted murmurs of "No, you're fine."

He wasn't fine. While he spoke loudly in general, we could barely hear him over all the external noise. "Actually, Luis," I piped up from the back of the room, "we do need you to put on a mic."

Luis wasn't doing anything to cultivate that fear. It arose simply by virtue of him being in the CEO role.

Our authority often makes us unapproachable, and that unapproachability fosters an isolation that rarely works to our benefit. To illustrate this dynamic in action, I sometimes use an exercise in corporate retreats taught to me by my colleague Jill Hufnagel. We assign one person in the group to be the "authority figure." Each of the other people in the group then have to hand that figure something that has some meaning or value to them. A shoe, a pair of glasses, their keys—doesn't matter what it is as long as it's a physical object upon which they depend in some way. As more and more items pile into the hands of the authority figure, a curious thing happens. Not one person ever offers to help them hold the objects, which the group quickly realizes symbolize the myriad needs and expectations of the team. No one even pulls up a table to make it easier for the authority figure. Then, once the authority figure has a full armload of stuff, I ask them to tie my shoe in a very fussy, demanding way. Again, no one offers to hold the goods while they do so. To finish the exercise, the authority figure then has to give each item back to its owner one by one, remembering who gave them which object. Still, no one helps, and of course, the authority figure almost never asks for help.

Authority is a badge of honor that few, if any, dare to question. The controversial Milgram experiment, done at Yale University in the 1960s, shed an unflattering light on just how deeply authority obedience is ingrained in our psyche. Participants were ordered by an actor posing as a scientist to administer electric shocks to hidden subjects if that person gave an incorrect answer to a question (these subjects were not in actuality receiving the shocks but reacted as though they were). The alleged shock recipients let out cries of pain, some begging that the study be halted. Despite these protests, dismissed by the study administrators with a mandate to "please continue," 65 percent of the participants complied all the way up to delivering what they believed were the maximum-level shocks. The leader of this study, social psychologist Stanley Milgram, concluded that people will obey authority out of fear or a desire to be cooperative, despite their own better judgment.

While controversial, this study unearthed some uncomfortable truths about our habituated response to power. Power dynamics are so ingrained in our muscle memory that we barely see them. But just as we must revise our definition of success, we must examine power dynamics if we want to thrive in an authority role.

Adjusting to the Spotlight

One day I was standing in line at the grocery store by the rack of celebrity magazines. In front of me were two men who looked to be in their early twenties. One picked up a copy of *People* with a famous female celebrity on the cover and visibly sneered.

"Oh, man," he said to his friend. "This b-tch has teeth like a horse."

I didn't know this actor personally, but immediately my heart hurt for her. What had she done to invite such ugly commentary?

Nothing, other than daring to step into the spotlight. We tend to think money, fame, prestige, and power cast a rosy glow, and very often they do. At the same time, whether you're a celebrity or the boss, the spotlight can also be more glaring than we expect. The same spotlight that illuminates your accomplishments can, at times, feel uncomfortable and intrusive.

One of the pivotal times I came to understand this was back when my colleague George became a partner at Microsoft. He was irritated by how curious people on his team were about his personal life. "Why do they care what kind of car I drive?" he asked me, incredulous. He was particularly annoyed to learn this had been a hot topic in the break room.

I happened to know the inquisitive chatter went beyond what kind of car George drove. There was speculation about why his wife traveled to Switzerland so often (*Plastic surgery? Weight loss clinic?*) and which way his politics leaned. There's nothing out of the ordinary here; people by nature are keenly interested in the personal business of those they report to. While on the one hand this curiosity can feel intrusive, there's another way to look at this that serves you better than clamming up and sequestering yourself.

For the most part, people want to know this stuff to connect with you. They want to know you're human, perhaps even to bond over a shared interest or other special commonality. This desire for connection through common ground goes beyond simply wanting to be chummy. As actor Alan Alda relayed in his book on the science of communicating, *If I Understood You, Would I Have This Look on My Face?*, scientists at Harvard utilized MRI scans to show that people were better able to read others' states of mind when they saw similarities between themselves and the other person.

Of course, sometimes the spotlight can feel more like an unwanted X-ray of your innards. When I worked at Microsoft, a lot of people told me they admired me. With that admiration, I developed a little bit of a following, which I didn't realize included some of my friends at the company. I was talking once with my colleague and friend Cindy about how my husband Matthew's beard scissors had been confiscated by airport security the previous weekend when we were on our way to North Carolina. Somehow, in a funny bonding moment, it came out that I also sometimes used his scissors to trim my hair when I was on the road and didn't have time for a proper haircut.

"I knew it!" Cindy exclaimed. "I *told* Gwen that you shared Matthew's beard scissors for that!"

To be clear: Gwen was the sitter Cindy hired for her child. Why was she talking about my personal hygiene with her child's caregiver who didn't even know me?

We can thank everything from social media to the rise of celebrity culture for this possessiveness. People feel free to share opinions about the personal lives of anyone who stands in the spotlight—including you, as the boss. That spotlight—warm or harsh—isn't going anywhere. Just like the rise in expectations, it gets turned on the instant you step onto the big stage and stays on in perpetuity. All eyes are on you, every decision debated, every comment magnified, every minor flaw illuminated in high definition. As one of my clients who appears often on television remarked, "Every piece of spinach stuck in my teeth now becomes a meme." Those who report to you will always be watching, trying to ascertain personal information about who you are, what you like and what you don't, how they can connect with you, and yes, sometimes, how they can use and trade on insight about you to their best advantage. Your work now isn't to avoid the glare, but to hone your ability to shine when it's cast upon you.

CHAPTER TWO

Common Boss Myths and Mistakes

Exceptionally brilliant and analytical, Chung had methodically worked his way up to a director role, which he was due to begin in a week. Chung's company offered coaching for their senior managers, and he requested we work together. Chung appeared at our first meeting with his e-notebook in hand, calmly poised with his stylus ready. When I asked him what he hoped to gain from our sessions, his answer was clear: "I want to bring you on as my thought partner and coach now so I can grow and succeed in this new role."

Chung is something of an anomaly in my world. When my phone rings, it is most often a call from clients who are struggling. Sometimes they're in hot water, having said or done something that has jeopardized their career or is threatening to take them out entirely. Or they reach out because they're feeling thwarted, knotted in conflicts, overwhelmed, or unfulfilled. Other times, it isn't the client themselves but their head of HR calling out of desperation.

Nandi was one such client. On the heels of scathing feedback from her peers and her team, Nandi came to our meeting chastened, concerned, and confused. During her exceptional rise from a great researcher in chemical engineering to the provost of a large university on the West Coast of the U.S., she had never been told she was failing—until now.

With no idea what she was doing wrong, Nandi was now too nervous to say anything during her manager's staff meetings or make decisions on behalf of her team. Instead of jumping right to the feedback she'd gotten and asking her to do the opposite of what people were criticizing her for, I started digging for the assumptions she had made as she started this role.

We quickly discovered Nandi had bought into common boss myths that bring many managers to me. She had thought of herself as a "good boss" and now could only consider herself a "bad boss." This hobbled any progress she wanted to make as her confidence took a dive with the new negative label. As an introvert and an early riser, Nandi liked to spend time thinking through ideas on her own and then getting down to business the minute meetings started. She also prided herself on taking on a heavy workload and hitting every target, every deadline, and being herself. Nandi considered what she labeled superficial chit-chat with her colleagues a waste of their time and hers. When complaints about her management style filtered up to her, Nandi would wave them off with justifications. In other words, Nandi had bought into all four of the most pervasive boss myths we'll be exploring in this chapter, along with the mistakes those myths generate.

When you think things are going according to plan but have a niggling sense something is not quite right, jumping into action without first examining the beliefs driving those actions is ill-advised. It's like locking the cookie cabinet to keep yourself from indulging without assessing what's sending you running for the sugary snacks in the first place. You know how that story ends, and it usually isn't with you happily digging into a plate of carrot sticks.

What boss myths have you bought into, and how have myths tangled you in common boss missteps, or how might they in the future?

Myth #1: There Are "Good" and "Bad" Bosses

As a trained engineer, I love nothing more than a proven system. Sometimes I like to fantasize coming up with a formula for being a "good boss" that I can replicate to flawless success. Everyone who gets promoted to management level could reproduce it, and *voilà*—best boss ever! I could ride off into the sunset and drink fruity cocktails with parasols in them on a beach somewhere, content in the knowledge that I'd saved the world from bad bosses forevermore.

Great fantasy, right?

Back here in reality, however, there is no one-size-fits-all formula for being a good boss. Buying into the myth that there are "good" and "bad" bosses perpetuates the fallacy that we are either one or the other, but the reality is more slippery than that. Just as no person is all good or all bad, the measure of a boss is neither binary nor fixed. "Bad bosses" are rarely bad people. In fact, most of them are good people with the best of intentions who unwittingly cross a tenuous dividing line between good intentions and bad behaviors. The pressing question is, what happens along the way to cause that slippage?

The first two clients I did 360s for both had a very hard impact on others. Logan was well-meaning and spoke of wanting to encourage his team, yet his 360 revealed he was seen as grumpy, impatient, and rude. Like Logan, Kara cared deeply about her team and their collective results, but many employees complained about her abruptness and tendency to make withering comments in response to suggestions. Both executives' admins were their "weather checks," or barometers of their moods that others would consult before approaching the boss. In our one-on-ones, I found both Logan and Kara to be wonderful people. They were kind, generous with their time, and gave a lot of thought to the needs of the individuals on their teams. The rough exterior they presented to their teams masked their determination to do right by their people. As a result of their outward spikiness, many people weren't at their best in front of either of them; several didn't want to work for them at all.

This got me curious. How can seemingly great human beings—who don't wake up in the morning thinking, *How can I demoralize the people I work with?*—still end up being the source of misery for their colleagues? They seem great in one setting, like our coaching conversations, but wreak havoc in others, such as when conducting daily business. This is when I began to unpack the nuances of how power and pressure can turn well-meaning, intelligent (and unaware) people into bosses from hell.

Far from being a fixed science, being a good boss is an art that is in constant revision, no matter how long you've been in that role. Learning to be a "good boss" is an ongoing process that requires the application of specific strategies and tools to manage pressure and power *in the moment*—or to be more accurate, in *every* moment. Anyone can be a good boss when the sun is shining, excellent work is flowing, profits are booming, and industry publications are raving. It's what you do when the thunder clouds roll in, and your team isn't running like a shiny, well-oiled machine, that determines which side of the "good boss/bad boss" line you land.

Coaching Consideration: Pause and Reflect

What would your biggest fans say about what it's like to work with you? What would your greatest detractors say?

Myth #2: Business Isn't Personal

Susan was the head of operations of a small company that had been recently bought by a larger conglomerate. The parent company had allowed the original, smaller firm to operate independently, until now. The operations team would remain under Susan's independent domain, but some of the back-office operations such as finance and HR were being integrated into the larger entity. As a result of these changes, key people had been exiting the organization.

People on Susan's team were understandably concerned. With each passing day, the number and urgency of calls and emails from people on her team increased; the inquiries were escalating to demands that they be told what was going on.

"What are you telling them?" I asked.

"I'm trying to keep things professional and telling them there's nothing to worry about, so they'll be able to stay focused on the work," she said, with a tiny shrug that belied her lack of confidence in that assurance.

As I relayed to Susan, telling someone who is concerned about the security of their livelihood not to worry is about as effective as telling someone who is terrified of spiders they shouldn't be afraid when a fat, hairy one is crawling up their leg. Feelings are feelings; it's pointless and patronizing to tell others what they should or should not feel. Plus, reassurances don't work. They make people more anxious. *Why is she telling me not to worry? There must be cause to worry; I wasn't worried before, but maybe now I should be?* Lastly, it's easy for her to say "don't worry" from her altitude; if she left, she'd receive a cushy exit packet, but her team certainly wouldn't.

Susan's mistake here wasn't that she wanted to give her team some peace of mind. It was glossing over the fact that *business is always personal*. We can't separate who we are in our work life from who we are in the personal realm. Yes, work demands a certain level of professionalism, and you can (and should) separate the two, but we show up to work as human beings, and events and interactions impact us. This is why empathy has become such a hot topic in the management world over the past decade. In the face of mounting pressures and stresses in today's workplace, business experts cite empathy as a crucial leadership skill, many touting it as *the* most crucial. We have only to look at the success of Microsoft CEO Satya Nadella, a notably empathetic executive credited for returning the tech giant's stock to growth status after nearly a decade of stagnation. As Nadella has stated, "My personal philosophy and my passion . . . is to connect new ideas with a growing sense of empathy for other people."

A recent Catalyst study by Tara Van Bommel, Ph.D., further showed the potency of managers' empathy. Employees who reported their managers as empathetic cited a significantly greater likelihood of being innovative and engaged. Those who felt their life circumstances were respected and valued were more likely to remain with the company. Also, when workers thought their supervisor expressed empathy, they reported far greater success juggling the competing demands of their personal and work lives.

Rather than dismiss or use reassurance to address the concerns of her team, I coached Susan to make a list of the all-too-human fears, uncertainties, and doubts they might be harboring but may not always state explicitly, then share that list with her team. That would assure them she was tuned in and had given thought to the position they were in. It would allow them to feel seen and heard. From there, she could speak to her own feelings on the matter while acknowledging that she did, indeed, occupy a different perch. Lastly, she would share openly what she knew and was allowed to pass along in terms of facts and data, to demystify the unknown as best she could.

If you're reading this and thinking, *Yeah, but I don't have time to waste worrying about every emotional paper cut of my team*, keep reading. The words *"yeah, but"* are both a valuable warning and an opportunity.

Coaching Considerations: Assess Your Approach
- What were you taught about the line between business and personal, and how has that informed your beliefs?
- How do you manage (e.g., embrace, dismiss, or process) your own emotions when a business situation hits a personal nerve?

Myth #3: *"Yeah, but"* Is a Justified Stance

"Yeah, but none of this applies to me."

"Yeah, but they just don't get it."

"Yeah, but I have too much going on to worry about what people think of me."

I could go on and on with the list of *"yeah, buts"* that pervade the thinking of high-level managers. You probably have one or two of your own that have bubbled up already as you read this. That's good news, because as I mentioned, *"yeah, but"* is a signal that you've hit upon a golden opportunity to see what you may have been blinded to thus far and where you can make a potent improvement in your management approach. That is, when you're willing to see it that way.

Always the smartest person in the room, Victor wasn't afraid to show it. He was the first to speak and commandeered every meeting. And like a fiery sausage in a New Orleans gumbo, he was not shy about simmering in self-applause while being spicy hot in his critique of others. Victor was buoyed by some of the wealthiest and most prominent thought leaders on the planet funding his company. He did whatever he thought was right—that sounds reckless, but he usually *was* right—without considering the effect of his unilateral moves on others. Toxic blame and raging tantrums were his modus operandi when presented with problems or less-than-dazzling reports from his team. Terrified of getting burned in the line of fire, they learned to hide burgeoning issues that would trigger him.

When I told Victor his 360 feedback unanimously crowned him an "asshole," he leaned back in his chair, lifted his feet onto the coffee table, interlaced his hands behind his head in the universal symbol of "I'm completely unfazed by what you're saying," and said with a smirk, "Sabina, please. I have been called an asshole ever since I was five. That's what makes me successful. People don't listen to nice people who do that touchy-feely garbage my HR director keeps trying to get me to do. They listen to me when I yell and curse and call them out. That's when they pay attention, when I deliberately lose my shit in meetings."

Managers like Victor aren't oblivious or ashamed of their bad behavior; they wear their noxious traits as a badge of pride. I've lost count of the number of people like Victor who take "you're an asshole" feedback as a compliment. With the results he was raking in and the high-profile attention he garnered in the business press, Victor had earned the right to be an asshole, right?

Dead wrong. Sorry, Vic.

Toxic behaviors like bullying, belittling, tantrums, off-color jokes, inappropriate comments (or worse) that might have been more accepted as business as usual a decade ago are no longer remotely acceptable, especially from those in power. We have only to conjure up the latest ethics scandal splashed across the media to prove that point. The days of "hear no evil, see no evil" are over, and business today is about treating one another with respect and understanding differences and boundaries. Thanks to social media, what used to be hidden is no longer. A study in 2019 by PwC showed that for the first time in two decades, scandals over bad behavior surpassed poor financial performance as the leading cause of chief executives' dismissals from the world's 2,500 largest public companies.

If I had to point to one characteristic all my clients have in common, it's a reluctance to jettison their damaging behaviors because they believe they've triumphed *because* of those very actions. While they believed these traits helped them rise, power and pressure at this new level have subverted those traits into behaviors that undermine their business results.

This confusion is understandable because *toxic work behavior stems from the same traits that make us stand out and help us win.* Determination and obstinance, confidence and arrogance, directness and callousness are flip sides of the same coin: to succeed at the top, you must adapt your behavior to come out with the winning toss. The sticking point is that the higher your rank, the more difficult it becomes to distinguish between good and bad expressions of your personality traits. The higher up the ladder you go, the harder it gets to monitor yourself and read nuance and know when you've tipped across the line.

Your success came *despite* these traits, not because of them. That's important to let sink in. I show clients the ways they've been achieving only a fraction of their potential to boost organizational results because they're wedded to these negative behaviors. That's when I really get their attention. From lack of delegation to poor communication to the absence of personal boundaries, their outcomes have *always* been hampered by behaviors they perversely consider essential to their success.

At least, that's when I get most of my clients' attention. Explaining this to Victor did nothing to budge him from his position. But after six months, the crescendo of negative feedback and comments on public forums like Glassdoor nudged Victor off his perch. He left the company, and other boards were reluctant to hire him as CEO of a new firm given his reputation.

Not all *"yeah, buts"* come wrapped in arrogance.

Daria was being groomed by her boss, the CEO, to be his successor. She had risen up the ranks superfast but felt hindered by a lot of resistance from her team. The results of her 360 showed that Daria came across as intolerant of slowness, incompetence, obtuseness—lower life-forms, in her book. Daria pushed back hard on her 360: "Okay, but we are a small company, we don't know if we'll make it, and we can't afford slackers or incompetence." Her *"yeah, but"* balloon quickly deflated when I pointed out that regardless of how carefully she hired, she would always end up with some B and C players in addition to the A players; that was just the law of numbers. Something shifted in her, and she nodded thoughtfully when I said, "Given that you have B and C players, unless you want to fire them all, we need to figure out how you get your B and C players to do their A work."

Daria regained her team's trust by asking more questions and leaning into what they had to say instead of cutting them off. She trusted others to figure the details out when she delegated an item. She even took care to rearrange her face to soften her habitual frown so as not to transmit unintended messages. Leaving behind her *"yeah, but"* allowed Daria to take a huge leap forward as a manager.

I'll leave you with a few other *"yeah, buts"* that are best jettisoned:

- *"Yeah, but I'm too valuable to be replaced."* No, you're not. I've heard *"yeah, buts"* from clients who thought the same thing and are now desperate to figure out where they went wrong while they hunt for a new job.

- *"Yeah, but my boss was hard on me . . . It's a rite of passage for my team to prove themselves."* When I was growing up in India, it was not uncommon in an arranged marriage for a mother-in-law to torture the young wife, in extreme cases even dousing her in kerosene and lighting her on fire if they ran through the money she'd brought from her dowry. These mothers-in-law would have gone through the same torture and fear themselves as young brides, perpetuating the abusive mentality. Is it a crime? Of course. While this may sound like a dramatic parallel, some bosses perpetuate a similar absurd line of thinking. Yes, you may have had a crappy, mean, or even abusive boss, but you hated it, so why would you want to inflict that same pain on someone else and perpetuate the problem? Moreover, times have changed, and passing along that toxicity is no longer okay. If humanity alone isn't enough to jolt you out of this *"yeah, but"* line of thinking, cancel culture will be only too happy to oblige.

- *"Yeah, but I know I'm right."* You very well might be. But also, is there more that perhaps you haven't considered? Often when we think we're right, there are many other ways to see the situation that we might not have considered yet. As you'll read about in Part Three, this *"yeah, but"* is a signal that you have fallen into the trap of righteousness.

- *"Yeah, but this is just how I am."* This one is so pervasive and so wrong that it gets its own myth. Read on.

Coaching Consideration: "Yeah, but" as an Invitation

The improv practice of "yes, and" is a way to hold on to your beliefs *and* lean into the territory beyond your perspective. What if every "yeah, but" that comes up for you was converted into an invitation to consider "yes, and"? As in, "Yes, I'm having serious doubts about what you're saying, Sabina, *and* let me listen with curiosity to your perspective." You already know "yeah, but" is a dead end, but where might "yes, and" take you?

Myth #4: Authenticity Is Singular

As a financial manager for high-net-worth individuals, Thomas had a talent for winning over major, blue-chip customers that impacted his company's revenue to the tune of millions of dollars. He was viewed by many in his industry as a rising star; if he could just overcome a few things (or so said his boss, who sent him my way), he could easily become a Fortune 50 CEO someday.

The sticking point was his temper. Key players on Thomas's team were having allergic reactions to the fits he threw anytime someone delivered an update he didn't like. In addition to the usual adjectives that show up in the 360 of a "yeah, but" personality, like "blunt," "dismissive," or "arrogant," Thomas's revealed a nasty streak that he let fly at the slightest provocation. As with Victor, the phrase "loses his shit" showed up multiple times connected to tales of whiteboard erasers being thrown and spittle flying.

Thomas was aware that he was hotheaded; this was feedback he'd heard again and again throughout his life. As the youngest of six siblings, his fieriness ensured his voice was heard among the energetic squabbling. When I delivered the results of Thomas's 360 to him, his reaction was prompted not by the arrogance of *I'm a big-swinging you-know-what, so I get to act this way*, but resignation.

"I know my outbursts cause problems, Sabina," he sighed, rubbing his hand across his meticulously clipped beard. He was frank in disclosing that his unmodulated temper had cost him his marriage as well as several thousand dollars in speeding tickets for cursing out the cops who pulled him over. "But what can I do? That's just how I am. I have to be authentic, don't I?"

Boom. There it was. The word that's tripped up hundreds of my clients and undoubtedly caused the downfall of many a manager.

Here's why: there is no such thing as absolute authenticity.

That's right. Pure authenticity is a complete fallacy, because none of us shows up in exactly the same way in every aspect of our lives. Each of us is endowed with dozens of different roles and has varying sides we channel based on the roles we play. We have multiple identities that we step in and out of over the course of a single day. Some of mine, for instance, are coach, public speaker, author, mother, wife, South Asian woman, friend, learner, and extrovert. When I show up in my role as a wife, I am authentic in my commitment to being helpful when my husband needs me, prioritizing time with him, and being unfiltered and real. When I show up as a public speaker, I maintain my commitment to being "real," but I prioritize showing up in a prepared and polished way. As a learner, I thrive on alone time with an absorbing book, and as an extrovert, I crave brainstorming with others like it's oxygen. Which one of those is truly "me"? All of them. As founder of the Zen Hospice Movement and author of *The Five Invitations: Discovering What Death Can Teach Us About Living Fully*, Frank Ostaseski writes, "Life asks us to continually adapt. Roles, like most things, are fluid."

The word "authentic" is a tired buzzword we trot out to justify all kinds of behaviors that we either are afraid to let go of or simply don't know how to modulate. When my younger son was three years old, a business associate of mine came over for dinner. He was a large man with a stomach that protruded over his belt. Ziven toddled over to him, poked him straight in the belly button with his finger, and loudly proclaimed, "Looks like you have to go potty!"

Was my son being authentic? Absolutely. But he was also being a toddler. His was an unfiltered, instinctual reaction to what he was see-ing. There's a charming purity to toddlers for that very reason, even if it sometimes makes their parents wince in mortification. Part of our job as parents is to teach our children the refinements and nuances of civilized human interaction; we don't expect them to be born equipped with the capacity that enables us as adults to size up a situation and make a considered choice about how to respond.

Look, we *all* have childish internal reactions and impulses some-times. Who among us hasn't wanted to call a maddeningly slow, pencil-pushing bureaucrat an unkind name or stomp their feet and scream because they didn't get the high-profile assignment they wanted? That's totally normal and natural. And what's also normal and natural for adults is to acknowledge those impulses *and then consciously decide if acting on them is aligned with our values.*

That's the key difference between authenticity and integrity. Authenticity is primal, but integrity demands that we take a beat and assess whether our primal instincts are serving our present-day inten-tions. The Shakespearian wisdom of "to thine own self be true" has much merit, but in the modern world we've distorted authenticity and wield it as an "enlightened" excuse not to do the grown-up work of calibrating our actions to align with our intentions.

A lot of times when people refer to authenticity they really mean "integrity." They are talking about values. But values are never singular; we all hold competing values and must make trade-offs. Being a caring mother and being a good citizen can come into conflict if I can't afford the medication my child needs to save their life. If I see a pharmacy I know has that medication, you bet I'm going to want to break in and steal it. It's not a choice I make easily, but it's about prioritizing being a mother.

We all have competing priorities pulling at us all the time. Each one feels very real and very authentic to who we are. One conflict that many busy people face is the competing commitments to their physi-cal fitness and to their job. To make space for both in our jam-packed lives, we need to prioritize one over the other. We can't always choose to give up our workouts in favor of getting a few extra hours of work done; otherwise our health suffers. Nor can most of us hit the gym for four hours in the middle of every workday and still do our jobs at optimum effectiveness. Wiser minds know that at different times we need to rank one over the other.

Back to Thomas. I knew that besides being authentic, being respected by his team was a core value for him: a hot button. One anecdote that showed up in his 360 was the time he harshly chewed out a junior associate in front of the entire staff for arriving late to a meeting. In the split second before he exploded, though not conscious of it yet, Thomas was faced with a choice: he could either indulge his "authenticity" and throw a tantrum about how this associate was disrespecting his time and authority, or he could prioritize comporting himself as an executive worthy of the trust and respect he values and discuss the matter privately with the person after the meeting. Both were honest expressions of his values; the question was which one he would choose at that moment.

Authenticity stems from our values, but it is never singular. What's authentic for us in one circumstance may be very different than what's true for us in another. We make choices all the time. When someone shouts racist comments at my family as we are walking down an empty city street late at night, that's not the time for me to stand up for racial equity. That's when I prioritize the safety of my family over commitment to social justice.

Authenticity is also never static, because the definition of who we are changes as we progress through life. Your five-year-old authentic self isn't the same as your fifty-year-old authentic self. What matters to you is not static. As former rocket scientist and author of *Awaken Your Genius* Ozan Varol wrote, "Just because a younger version of you dreamt a dream doesn't mean you're forever tied to it. The 35-year-old you has little in common with the 25-year-old you. If you have any doubts about that, check out your older social-media posts. Once you're done wincing at those captions and those outfits, ask yourself, 'Why live by the choices of that person?'"

Telltale signs that you're circling the authenticity trap are phrases such as "That's just how I am," "I'm not the kind of person who," and "That's the way I've always done things, and it's worked for me." I often tell clients who take refuge in this language that they've become a one-trick pony. It pisses them off, and I get it. No one likes to hear that they aren't multidimensional. But if you insist you must do things *this* way because it's your formula or your nature, that makes you a hammer and everything else a nail. Ninety-five percent of the time your formula or your nature may work brilliantly for the occasion, but what about the 5 percent when it doesn't? What about the 5 percent of the time when it's not a nail in front of you, but a chair? Even more importantly, what are you missing out on or hiding from by insisting on remaining a hammer and a hammer only? If Thomas had chosen not to berate his direct report, he would have had time to be curious about *why* the associate was late. Or by avoiding the scolding, Thomas might have found the associate much more engaged and positive at the meeting. Actions have consequences. By trying new tactics, we learn new things.

As London Business School professor Herminia Ibarra outlines in her book *Act Like a Leader, Think Like a Leader*, clinging to the notion of authenticity can be a barrier to growth or an excuse for staying safely tucked inside the margins of our comfort zones. True, much of what you do as a hammer, so to speak, has made you a success. It is indeed who you are—or, at least, who you have been. But if you insist on staying the same and clinging to "that's just who I am," then that's who you're ever going to be. New level, new view—and yes, sometimes that means a new evolution of you.

Please don't misunderstand: I am not suggesting authenticity is slippery or that you do anything that is misaligned with your values. None of this is to imply you should be disingenuous. Rather, I'm suggesting there are always competing values, and we are always making choices.

The upshot here is not to let the smoke screen of past "authenticity" stand in the way of your future growth. Change is hard. Believe me, I get it; my entire career is based on helping people make healthy and necessary changes against the strong pull of resistance. If you remember that what matters more is aligning your actions with your values, you'll be able to more effectively step out of the "that's just how I am" box and move into more productive expressions of your integrity.

Coaching Consideration: Identify Your Integrity Denominators

- What roles do you play in your life, and how do you show up in each one?
- What is consistent about how you show up in each? What's different?
- What are the underlying values that inform the behaviors in the key roles you play?

CHAPTER THREE

The Obscuring Effect of Power

Tall, clean-shaven, and impeccably dressed, with a charming smile and a VP position at a rising tech security firm, Adam was the outward picture of a well-liked manager. He consistently delivered awesome business results, shredded the competition, brought in projects ahead of deadlines, and dazzled customers. No one in his industry was surprised when he was recognized as "one to watch" by a prominent business publication. Adam's performance earned him a promotion, placing him in charge of a multimillion-dollar product development team. Like so many über-performing executives I work with, Adam believed being an extraordinary businessperson naturally meant he was an exceptional manager. Great is great, right?

Then he got the call to come to his boss's office.

Amped up by a few record-breaking recent triumphs, Adam strode down the hall smiling his high-wattage smile, certain he was about to be promoted yet again or, at the very least, praised. He quickly deflated when his boss instead launched into a reproach about the number of complaints she'd been fielding about her star executive. Yes, Adam's outward business results were stupendous, but inside the walls of his organization, it seemed no one wanted to work with him. His boss made it clear that despite his outstanding work, Adam was becoming a liability as a boss. He was instructed to turn around his behavior—and fast.

As authors Martin Griffin and Jon Mayhew write in *Storycraft,* "Often the best villains are the ones who are convinced they are doing good." Adam was what I call an *innocent saboteur*—a well-meaning boss who engages in what they believe is success-generating behavior that is actually toxic to their team and their own career. Adam blithely bullied others in the sincere belief that this was the best way to generate better performance. He used sarcasm and insults to "motivate," jokes to soften the blow of those insults and "build camaraderie," and micromanagement to "mentor." But his methods were backfiring.

Adam's 360 was one of the worst I'd ever conducted, peppered with four-letter words, gripes about his inappropriate jokes and belittling jabs, and complaints about his gross lack of respect or appreciation for his team. He was universally considered "an arrogant asshole." The kicker was that he had no clue.

At heart, Adam was a good guy who genuinely thought his management tactics were on point. He had no idea how negatively his go-to behaviors were experienced by those he worked with, or the extent of the damage he was inflicting. Because no one dared not to laugh at his jokes in his presence, Adam thought his team appreciated his humor and believed they understood his jabs as playful motivation. It's never easy for my clients to receive difficult 360 feedback, but the crushed look on Adam's face particularly pained me. He was floored to learn how many of his peers and team who exalted him to his face excoriated him behind his back.

Adam meant well and, like many of my clients, was well-versed in the research on "best practices" for effective management. Yet he still fell into a troublesome divide I refer to as a *Power Gap.* There is a normal and healthy distance that exists between someone in an authority role and those who work for them. When that distance widens too much, however, a dangerous chasm of a Power Gap opens. Without knowing it, we can tumble in and unknowingly succumb to "bad boss" behaviors for one simple reason: *power blinds us.*

Power Gaps are tricky territory, rife with common human needs and emotions around authority. The borders of these gaps are outlined by the gravitas of your title and the power you now have over the professional destinies of those who report to you. You might know this intellectually but don't live with the realities of it every day, like the ever-present scepter of your authority constantly hanging over your direct reports. In your hands you hold control of their salaries and bonuses, whether they get promoted or not, what projects they work on and what they are excluded from, and what your superiors think of them.

As you'll discover more in Part Three, where we'll identify and unpack the most common Power Gaps and how to avoid them, you may not see the issues that arise when you're ensconced inside one. But rest assured, those who work for you certainly do and feel their effect. You won't know if or when you've slid into a Power Gap, because the walls are thickened with the cushion of praise, intimidation, and all the human dynamics stirred up in the face of authority. Nestled inside, you won't see what you did to wedge dangerous distance between you and your team, nor be aware of what's driving you. You certainly won't hear crucial feedback that would enable you to course correct in real time.

You become blind to your management missteps because no one is willing to tell you what they really think. Adam's tasteless jokes, which no one dared not to laugh at, were meant to forge wink-wink bonding with his team but, in fact, inspired nudge-nudge eyerolls behind his back. The driving energy he activated to close deals was experienced as a blunt instrument of bullying for his team. Wrap this all up in the padded protection from honest feedback that he was swathed in, and you can see how Adam was blind to the impact of his behaviors.

Oh, and you probably also won't really *want* to hear honest feedback, because, well . . . it's pretty comfy inside that gap. That's where our deep-seated hungers for love, adoration, validation, and respect get subconsciously fed and further insulate us from reality. When our team agrees with our ideas, our craving for validation is met. When we swoop in to fix problems, we feel needed. When they appreciate our efforts, we are loved. When they praise our decisions, we are respected. We'll keep doing what we do to get our needs met, even if unbeknownst to us those behaviors are sinking our chances for success. If you feel a *"yeah, but"* coming on, that's normal. Our primitive wiring to feed our unconscious hungers overrides rational thought that says, "I'm not that needy."

Even if we do have a few brave souls in our midst who will give it to us straight, there's a good chance we've built up plenty of defenses to justify why we're right and they're just being petty, complaining, lazy, obtuse, substandard, and flat-out wrong. Blaming others gets us out of having to take responsibility and change our ways, and changing our habits is among the most challenging of human endeavors. This is precisely why I always let my clients stew in their own juices for two weeks after I deliver difficult 360 results; it takes at least that long for their human defenses to calm down so that they're willing to see the impact of their behaviors, accept where they may be complicit, and return willing to make real changes for the sake of their and their teams' corporate survival.

Through our work together, Adam learned how to collapse the Power Gap that threatened to tank his career. He stopped the tasteless jokes. He pulled back from micromanaging by trusting his direct reports to run their teams without intrusion and replaced the "motivational" sarcasm with positive feedback. With the Power Gap narrowed, his team felt comfortable giving him unvarnished feedback so he knew immediately when to course correct, and was now armed with the tools to do so. Two years after we began working together, I re-interviewed his team, and the same colleagues who gave scathing feedback in his first 360 now sang his praises, declaring him (and again, I quote) "1,000 percent better."

Then there's Stella.

Like Adam, Stella was a well-intentioned rainmaker who was promoted to a position of authority, unaware that her go-to behaviors as a solo driver on a fast ascent were thwarting her best efforts as a manager. Unlike Adam, however, Stella's behaviors weren't necessarily toxic—they were just distorted by a Power Gap.

Stella was the first woman in her family to go to university. Not just any university, but as an honors student on full scholarship at Harvard. She graduated at the top of her class and snagged a coveted position in the cosmetics industry. Over the next two decades, Stella's rise had been meteoric. The cornerstone of her success was a trifecta of hard work, hyper-attention to detail, and speed. She was first to take ownership of a problem and applied a singular laser focus to deliver flawless results consistently ahead of schedule. When Stella came to me, she was the right-hand person to the CEO of a $2 billion company.

The air pressure in the conference room seemed to change when this five-foot-nothing dynamo walked in for our first meeting. "Walked" isn't exactly the right word; Stella zipped through space at a tempo two beats ahead of everyone else and talked at an equally fast clip. She arrived at that first meeting armed with her list of frustrations: she was overwhelmed but didn't delegate because no one on her team could do the work as quickly as she could, the corporate culture was sluggish, Stella was mired in internal politics and annoyed because she had to read every tea leaf before making a move. All these facts were true. Also true was that her team was starting to dwindle both in headcount and productivity. Stella was calling on the same high-octane skills that had always driven her successes, so what was going wrong now?

New level, same actions, different consequences. Racing forward at the same breakneck pace she had when she was a solo driver, Stella's trademark mixture of speed and hyper-attention to detail was now leaving her team choking in the dust.

Stella had risen to a position of authority without fully appreciating that she had veered into an entirely new reality where nothing was as it had been (see Myth #1: There Are "Good" and "Bad" Bosses).

She was still the extraordinary worker she had always been, but the traits she relied on to get to the top were now casting distinctly different shadows. Stella's particular blind spot was not knowing that *power skews how our traits and behaviors are seen and felt by others.* You can change absolutely nothing about who you are and how you make your brand of magic happen, but the day after your promotion, your words and actions are read differently. With your promotional transplant, the tenacity that propelled you upward is now interpreted by others as obstinance. Your trademark might have been directness; now, however, it's read as callousness. A self-starter becomes a selfish limelight-hog. And once again, inside the insulated echo chamber of the Power Gap, you won't know it.

Stella's drive for warp speed was interpreted by her team as an insensitivity to what it took to get a job done. Add in the snippiness that erupted when her pressure gauge ran too high, and things went off track. Just as I did not see where I'd veered off track years before, Stella couldn't see any of this. So she kept doing what she'd always done, unwittingly tripping up herself and her team.

Stella learned how to illuminate the blind spots that were impeding the results she wanted and impacting the people she managed. She didn't need to move faster and do more to compensate for her team and her expanded responsibilities, but to rethink her elevated role. Her work was no longer to burrow into every tiny detail, but to zoom out and think strategically. Strategy, not speed, was her new superpower. We empowered her with the tools to course correct by effectively sharing responsibility, mapping and calibrating her prized traits so they worked for rather than against her, and not wearing herself and her team down. Most importantly, Stella learned the diagnostic tools to prevent future blind spots from reopening.

When it comes to managing others, we rationally know what to do (or, at the very least, we know where to find the resources that list those best practices). It's what *not to do* that we don't know, and that can sabotage our efforts. Part Three outlines the most pervasive Power

Gaps, to equip you with the awareness of what not to do so you don't unwittingly fall in.

Coaching Consideration: The Power Gap Distortion

Take a moment and think about the traits you most prize about yourself and hold as essential to your success. Now consider how the *expression* of these traits might be construed by those who work for you through the prism of power dynamics. Some of the most common Power Gap distortions include:

- Direct / Callous
- Confident / Arrogant
- Strategic / Manipulative
- Detail-oriented / Micromanaging
- Determined / Obstinate
- Disciplined / Rigid
- Focused / Unapproachable
- Calm / Uninterested

CHAPTER FOUR

The Hidden Impact of Pressure

Abraham Lincoln once said, "Nearly all men can stand adversity, but if you want to test a man's character, give him power." I have the utmost respect for the sixteenth president of the United States, but I beg to differ. Power blinds us to the impact of our actions, but it's not power that corrupts a person's character. It's pressure.

Left unchecked, pressure makes monsters of us all.

How many times, in a time crunch or in overdrive to deliver, have you been brusque, dismissive, or even outright explosive? None of us is immune. Under enough pressure and without the right systems in place to manage it, anyone's inner monsters come out to play. Remember, there are no purely good or bad bosses—just bad behaviors forged under pressure.

Power distorts how our traits are seen and experienced by others, but pressure transmutes these traits. Our best qualities grow ugly fangs that we sink into anyone in our way. When pressure exceeds our capacity to manage it, our guardrails disappear. Our directness isn't just read as insensitivity—we actually *become* insensitive. When we are squeezed by pressure, our confidence takes a genuine turn into arrogance as we lose patience and humility. We just don't see these slipups because, as you now know, power blinds us to them. We almost never see repercussions of our blown pressure gauge until it's too late.

In an analysis of twelve-thousand-plus pages of data I have accumulated across thousands of interviews, the number one stated weakness of bosses is a tendency to be hard on others. In other words, bosses come across as bullies and jerks who tank people's morale and performance. The fine print on those behaviors includes inappropriate drama, being overly assertive, demanding, dictatorial, insecure, too focused on themselves and quick to react, just to name a few. These behaviors arise as a direct result of unmanaged pressure. It's really that simple—and that complex.

As you rise in position and the distance between you and those who work for you increases, so does the pressure. Regardless of whether you stand on the world stage, run a company of ten, or have stepped up to chair the school committee for the holiday concert, pressure comes at you from all angles. Common limitations like a lack of time or resources require you to think strategically while the clock is ticking and myriad personalities are campaigning for their best interests. Moreover, next-level roles require making crucial, leadership-level decisions that can have far-reaching consequences. You're called upon to strategize the big picture while juggling the personalities and performance issues of your team and operational administration, not to mention keeping a cool head under the blistering effects of the white-hot spotlight.

When pressure rises, our ability to think clearly and modulate our behavior tanks. Unless we increase our ability to manage it, pressure can easily trigger reactivity. *I'm late ... I'm in trouble ... I'm unliked ...* all these internal narratives in response to external forces bring out the worst in us.

Under enough pressure and without the right emotional strategies, even a normally thoughtful, kind person will slip up and engage in regrettable behavior. I'll confess I'm not proud of a certain appendage I've waved or the verbal vomit I've spewed when I'm running late to a meeting and a car cuts me off on my way there. Get me on a good day, when I'm well rested and not under pressure, though, and I will pull over to help a stranded driver.

Bosses don't become jerks overnight because they were awarded a fancy title. No one wants to become a toxic manager. The slip into "bad boss" behavior occurs when the dueling headwinds of power and pressure collide. Power blinds us to our behaviors, while pressure corrupts our ability to navigate what I call the Pressure Pitfalls, i.e. the mistakes we become vulnerable to when pressures run high.

As the person in charge, all eyes are on us, and that triggers something deep in our encoded DNA. That "something" is almost always a deep-seated fear—fear of being not liked, of being wrong or not perfect, of being found out as an imposter, of being laughed at, criticized, or rendered irrelevant. As I've said, no one is all good or all bad, but pressure and the psychological mechanisms it triggers certainly have a hefty impact on whether our inner Dr. Jekyll or Mr. Hyde comes out to play.

Mr. Hyde, by the way, doesn't always show up as an evil monster. Plenty of versions of this alter ego emerge when our strategies are not adjusted to meet elevated pressures. My client Jorge, for instance, turns into a grade-A avoider. He'll let important decisions pile up, calls go unanswered, and emails be ignored, all while telling himself he just needs to get a leg up on his work before getting back to everyone (which of course he never does). Ines turns into a character we've dubbed "Bad Cop," who dons a proverbial uniform and polices every detail with a brusque chilliness that makes her team wither.

If you're thinking, *But I do my best work under pressure*, I hear you, and there is absolutely merit to that. Pressure, by definition, is the force that moves something out of inertia into motion. A deadline to deliver can sharpen our thinking and drive performance. Countless clients have told me they are more productive when under stress; many find high-stakes moments exhilarating. What I'm referring to here, however, isn't one deadline or even a few high-level expectations. This is not just episodic pressure; it's sustained and vast amounts of pressure, from all directions, with no letup ever because there are always eyes on you. It is the unmanaged pile of expectations and demands that come at us all day, every day and open up deep pitfalls into which we can easily tumble and become trapped.

Regardless of the size and scope of the pressures on us or the shape our inner monsters take, if we don't carefully mitigate the insidious effects of power and pressure on our behavior, our results will flatline. The damage starts with us. Besides the proven damage to our well-being, productivity, and job satisfaction, unmanaged pressure blurs our ability to think strategically—a serious problem when strategic thinking is the cornerstone of your job as a manager.

How well you do or don't manage pressure impacts more than just your ability to sleep well at night. Again and again, I have seen how the actions of one toxic manager can hobble the efforts of an army of peers and direct reports. Being forced to tolerate negative behavior puts others in a constant state of threat. As the guiding hand of your team, any chink in your armor protecting against pressure directly undermines the productivity, loyalty, and performance of your team, which in turn hinders results. Remember, it's not all about you anymore. Managing the pressure inherent to your elevated role *is now part of your elevated role.*

Scores of research studies show that outbursts from authority figures trigger a biological response in employees. This threat response is driven by the human brain's primal part, the amygdala, which has to immediately choose between attacking, running away, or becoming tiger chow. Daniel Goleman, author of *Emotional Intelligence,* coined the term "amygdala hijack" to describe this phenomenon. It's been proven time and again that productivity and performance take a nosedive when employees are under these kinds of amygdala hijacks. Just as one example, research done by an expert on work stress, YoungAh Park, showed a strong correlation between receiving rude, alarming, or otherwise triggering emails and employees' withdrawal from work the following week. Park noted the primitive drive for self-preservation:

"When you are under great stress, you tend to avoid your work as a means of conserving your energy and resources and staying away from stressors. It's self-preservation."

When the amygdala lights up, we are incapable of processing new information, analysis, or rational thought. Our brain doesn't do a great job of differentiating between the physical threat of a tiger in front of us and an emotional threat activated by a manager baring their teeth. Either way, we suffer from a brain drain, dropping our IQ by double digits. As neuroscience expert Dr. Jens Hartmann has pointed out, the effect of these hijacks is cumulative. The more often we are hijacked in this way, the more we assume the threat is here to stay, and the faster we get triggered the next time. And on and on the cycle of corruptive contagion goes.

In Part Four, I'll unearth the most common Pressure Pitfalls and give you the specific tools to navigate around them or, when necessary, out of them if you do unwittingly fall in. We can't avoid pressure, but we can escape its corrosive grasp and learn to thrive in the face of it.

BECOMING THE BOSS OF YOU

Have you ever felt as though your calendar, interruptions, and email run your life? That you're at the constant mercy of fire drills, leaving you feeling out of control, drained, and somehow further behind at the end of the day than when you started?

We all do from time to time.

Many clients come to our first meeting saying they feel overrun by the constant demands on their time and attention. They want to manage their teams to excellence, but often feel as though the deluge and demands are in charge rather than them. As I tell these clients, to become an effective boss you must first become the boss of you. This means learning how to manage yourself first, and *then* manage others.

Part Two sets the foundation for shifting from overrun to empowered.

CHAPTER FIVE

The Foundational Tools

The rest of this book is about surfacing the areas you need to manage within yourself and accessing the action tools to do so. In Parts Three and Four, we'll examine the Power Gaps and Pressure Pitfalls, and—most importantly—tools to successfully maneuver around them. Before we get to the diagnostics of where you may need to sharpen your managerial skills, however, we need to establish foundational habits to ensure the effectiveness of all the others.

This chapter introduces three foundational tools: Cost vs. Benefit Analysis, Micro Habits, and the Yes List. Implementing these throughout the chapters that follow will enable you to bypass the normal human resistance to change, move the needle through doable increments, and track your progress in an easy way that sets you up to succeed.

To Bypass Resistance: Cost vs. Benefit Analysis

If I asked you what percentage of people who get wheeled into the hospital needing emergency bypass surgery go on to make the prescribed lifestyle changes afterward, what would you say? Sixty percent? Fifty?

The answer is 10 percent. Ninety percent fail to make changes to their lifestyle habits, even though these adaptations could save them from having to repeat another painful, costly surgery in the future or, worse, dying of a heart attack.

This is only one of hundreds of studies that prove what any of us who have ever tried to make behavior changes know all too well: change is hard. From my professional perspective, why else would anyone give up their valuable time and money to hire an executive coach?

Beginning is the easy part. Fueled with resolve, we set off down the road of our new plan with the sparkling clarity of a sunshine-filled New Year's Day morning. But when pressure closes in and our automated habits clamor to be heeded, we inevitably run into resistance. As soon as we encounter a familiar cue (a budget cut, a snafu made by a direct report), we trigger a neurological cycle that author of *The Power of Habit* Charles Duhigg describes as the "habit loop." On high alert, our primitive brains signal, *Danger! Danger! Risk ahead!*, and we take the second step in the loop, automating to our familiar routine. This in turn provides us with whatever reward that habit brings us— comfort, control, emotional release, or cake—thereby closing the habit loop with us sealed inside.

The difference between succeeding and failing to make long-term adjustments to our behaviors comes down to the question of where we direct our attention. In other words, focusing on what we stand to gain or what we stand to lose. Robert Kegan and Lisa Laskow Lahey's "Immunity to Change" framework highlights how we all have competing commitments. We want to lose weight, but we also want to eat what we want and enjoy ourselves. We are committed to cleaning up our calendar to free up more time and mental space, but we are also committed to not disappointing anyone, or appearing busy and important, or whatever hunger is lurking in the shadows. That shadow motivation gets formed early in life as a survival mechanism, which we then carry as a roadblock into our adult lives.

As Marty Linsky and Ronald Heifetz point out, however, people don't fear change—they fear loss. Psychologists even refer to the five core fears—abandonment, loss of identity, loss of meaning, loss of purpose, and death—as "universal themes of loss." Cavepeople weren't afraid of saber-toothed tigers, per se; they were afraid of losing their lives being gnashed to bits by their ginormous teeth. We don't fear failure; we fear losing our identity and sense of meaning. Or if we fail publicly, we're afraid we'll lose respect or our status in the organization. Every change—even the very best ones—involves some kind of loss. Anyone who has ever moved in with a partner knows that the joy of cohabitation also comes with a bit of lost privacy and singular control over which way the toilet paper roll is hung. When we get promoted, we lose the familiarity of our old role, the comfort of being squarely in our high-performance wheelhouse, and the routine responsibilities to which we've become accustomed.

There is a powerful force calling us back to the status quo because people are so fearful of venturing into the unknown and losing the familiar. We gloss over that force, but it is often stronger than our will to change. What effectively gets us to change is *determining that what we stand to gain is greater than what we're giving up*. It's a straightforward cost/benefit analysis. That benefit is your "why"—your reason for committing to change in the first place. Resistance occurs when the cost feels more pressing than the gain, but when the benefit—aka your "why"—feels greater than the cost, then scaling over those resistance hurdles becomes easy.

Let's say, for instance, your goal is to lose weight. And that you love cake. I mean, who doesn't love cake? The lure of gooey, sweet frosting and fluffy layers can feel impossible to resist. As many nutritionists point out, however, identifying the *reason* to pass on that cake is what makes the difference between unconsciously stuffing your face and saying, "No, thank you." When the desire to feel better, fit into your clothes, and get healthy so you can be there for your family in the long term is made palpable, it offers a powerful counter to the siren call of sweets.

The key to succeeding in your application of the Cost vs. Benefit tool is to train your focus to remain on what you stand to gain rather than what you might lose. In the chapters that follow, for each tool, you'll find a cost vs. benefit equation to consider, which will fortify your commitment to your "why."

> **Coaching Consideration: We don't only feel loss with failure.**
> With every success come some casualties too. Consider whom or what you stand to lose if you succeed in making your desired behavioral change. How does that impact your commitment?

To Move the Needle: Micro Habits

The biggest mistake my clients make when attempting change is trying to implement a wholesale, top-to-bottom reset. Bill Gates once said, "Most people overestimate what they can achieve in a year and underestimate what they can achieve in ten years." What that means is go big but do it in a reasonable time frame. Complete transformation overnight is not realistic—and your lack of progress against your goal will discourage you. When participants in my workshops analyze their Time Portfolio (a tool you'll find on page 216), many are sobered to realize they're time-broke, focusing on less productive and meaningful activities and not on their key goals. As hard-charging Type A's, they immediately resolve to detox from all devices, chisel their bodies into shape with grueling daily workouts, and catch up on past commitments overnight. They aim to ingest the new macro habit in one giant gulp. Clearly, if it was as easy as that, they would have already reached these objectives, and many more. But change doesn't work that way, not change that sticks. Crash diets might squeeze us into a dress or tuxedo next week, but research shows that 70 to 90 percent of people gain their pounds right back, plus more. We want real, lasting change, not a spike-and-crash cycle.

Enter Micro Habits.

Micro Habits are big habits broken into ridiculously small steps.

They're the building blocks of new macro habits; in essence, a habit to create a habit. The two essential ingredients for a Micro Habit are:

1. Perform it daily
2. Keep it small

That's it. Daily, because you're carving new neural pathways that form only with repetition. Small, because they're tiny enough to sneak past our defense systems and start to inoculate us against change resistance.

This small initial step should take no more than one to two minutes to complete. I encourage clients to think of this as a limbo contest: How low can you go? Lower the bar for a new habit's size until it's so low you laugh out loud. Want to get in better shape and run a marathon, but the only marathon you currently engage in is a Netflix binge? Start by establishing a Micro Habit of putting on your sneakers once a day and walking up and down the steps of your front porch. Aiming to clean your messy closet? Start by folding one sweater. Looking to start a meditation practice? Begin with one mindful breath. It sounds absurd, but it works.

Here are a few real-life examples from my clients:

- After receiving some particularly stinging feedback in his 360 about tuning out in meetings if the topic did not directly apply to his department, Haoyu established a goal of listening better. His Micro Habit was to attend one meeting each day without devices.

- To temper her rescuer urges, Inge committed to a goal of once per day asking someone else for their ideas of how to solve a problem rather than jumping in with her superhero cape flying.

- To bypass his "do it perfectly or not at all" hurdle to keeping up with industry news, Joseph committed to reading just one paragraph in an industry publication each night.

- A chronic yes-sayer who was loath to miss out on anything (and therefore overburdened with work), Morgan's Micro Habit was to respond once per day with "Let me think about that and get back to you."

- To moderate her lightning-fast responses, which were generating misunderstandings, and instead become more intentional, Andrea established the daily morning habit of writing out one important problem she needed to tackle that day before checking her phone for messages and requests from others.

By being low stakes, Micro Habits are a safe experiment. They allow you to see what happens if you break the habit loop and step outside your comfort zone. Did the sky fall if you said no to one invitation? Did you miss out on anything that urgent if you did not check your email during one meeting?

The low-stakes nature of Micro Habits also bolsters our resilience. We build resilience through recovering from failure. Fall down, get up, repeat: that's the process for establishing better adaptive responses to pressure. It's also the way we learned how to walk when young. Did we give up and tell ourselves we were failures because we fell? We probably laughed and tried it again. It's the same way we build musculature now: stress the muscle and create tiny tears in the fibers, which then recover stronger and better equipped to lift heavier weights the next go-around. The process of recovering from failure also builds the prefrontal cortex—the area associated with regulating emotions and decision-making—and tamps down the amygdala—which triggers fight-or-flight reactivity. So failure is not necessarily a bad thing. Sociologist Dr. Christine Carter says unless we're willing to be bad at first, it's hard to feel good about adopting a new habit. With a Micro Habit we fail small and recover more easily.

When I introduce the practice of Micro Habits, clients will often scoff. They raise an eyebrow and say, "But Sabina, this is ridiculous. I can't do only one push-up a day!" That's when I know they've identified a true Micro Habit. If it feels utterly ridiculous, you're on target. Try this process right now:

1. Think of a goal you want to achieve. It can be anything, professional or personal.
2. Next, think of one step you can take to make progress on it.
3. STOP RIGHT THERE.
4. Now halve the size of that step, then slash it again, and then a little more.
5. Keep going until it almost takes more effort to write out the Micro Habit than it will take to do it. You might laugh at the size of this new habit. If you consider it too puny to share with anyone, you're there.
6. Now trying doing it every day without fail.

Making your new habit truly micro improves the odds you'll stick to it, because the only thing more ridiculous than this tiny habit is not accomplishing such a minuscule task. But the impact of those minuscule tasks adds up quickly. As author and columnist Arianna Huffington says, "By making very small changes, you have the power to change your life."

For the tools in the following chapters, I include a suggested list of Micro Habits to get you from where you are to where you want to be.

 Pro Tip: Don't Think, Just Do

Through a deep dive into neuroscience and habit loops, motivational speaker and author Mel Robbins established her groundbreaking "5 Second Rule." Here's how it works: The instant we get an instinct to move in a new direction, the brain's automatic wiring is activated; like a protective hawk, it swoops in to magnify risk, masquerading as self-doubt. You have exactly five seconds in between the thought and the triggering of your automated resistance that talks you out of it, so don't pause. Act. Count backward from five to one and then get down and do the one push-up. As Robbins says, "True change comes down to five-second windows."

Pro Tips for Succeeding in Micro Habits

1. **Change the scenery.** Switching venue has been proven to improve the chance of success in altering habits. Outside our usual surroundings, our brains disconnect from their automated wiring. Contextual cues in our familiar surroundings are triggers for automated habits. If you rarely eat Peanut M&Ms other than when you go to the theater but can think of nothing other than those crunchy colorful candies the minute you take your seat before the show starts, that's what I mean by a "contextual cue." Put this tip into practice by physically moving out of the space where the usual behaviors play out and choosing a new one in which to practice your Micro Habit. If your Micro Habit is to spend less time scrolling through your phone, for instance, and you generally do that while eating lunch at your desk, go sit in the cafeteria at lunchtime and talk to someone instead.

2. **Piggyback the habit.** Create new contextual cues by linking your Micro Habit to an existing routine. Learn one new word in a foreign language while brushing your teeth. Write your strategic intention for the day while drinking your morning

coffee. Do your one paragraph of reading on your train ride home.

3. **Track it.** After you complete your Micro Habit for the day, be sure to physically note its completion. See the Yes List tool on page 68 for more on how and why tracking progress in writing is key for changing habits.

4. **Stay small for longer than you think you need to.** Before you declare victory and increase the size of your new activity, hold steady for at least four weeks to fully ingrain the habit. If we extend our reach too fast, we will fail more readily and then give it up the next day. Productive failure is one thing; setting oneself up for futility is another. Leave yourself looking forward to the next day, excited to pick up where you left off rather than feeling too discouraged to tackle what felt onerous the day before. Many of my über-successful clients fail at some point in their Micro Habit journey because they try to go from micro to medium to macro too fast. If you find yourself in this situation, simply go back to the original micro-sized habit.

5. **If you're not succeeding, go smaller.** Slash and then slash again. The smaller the habit, the greater your likelihood to stick with it and build the stamina to keep going. Again, if that feels ridiculous to you, remember that a ridiculously small change is better than none at all.

To Facilitate Progress: The Yes List

I walked into our bedroom one evening to find my husband Matthew pacing up and down the length of the room.

"What on earth are you doing?" I asked.

Matthew glanced down at his Garmin watch, and I laughed. I should have known. "I'm at nine thousand, four hundred steps today," he said. "No way am I going to sleep without getting to ten thousand!"

Working with individuals who perform at high levels (not to mention being married to one), I'm accustomed to hearing about people walking around their dining tables until they hit their step goal for the day or jumping in place to trigger the activity counter for the hour. One client confessed to placing her watch on the dryer so she'd accrue steps through the machine's vibrations; another asked his wife to take his watch on her run.

Gamifying our exercise has given legs to our fitness goals, underscored by tons of research. Recording our goals and tracking our progress have been proven in countless studies to exponentially increase rates of success in establishing any new habit, most specifically those centered on our personal well-being. A meta-analysis of 138 studies of nearly twenty thousand participants, published by the American Psychological Association, showed that the more often a subject monitored their progress (e.g., hourly or daily), the greater the likelihood they would succeed.

This is why I have my clients create a daily Yes List. A Yes List is a way to track your habits, starting with the micro and expanding in time all the way up to macro sustained practices. It's a daily tracker to create accountability for any of the tools you're deploying. If you're groaning at the thought of a daily action, I assure you this will take you no more than sixty seconds per day.

The steps to creating and implementing a Yes List are simple:

1. **Choose 3–5 Micro Habits to focus on.** Five is the maximum to ensure you'll stick with this.
2. **Create your weekly grid.** You can either create this grid by hand or print out the blank template on my website: www .sabinanawaz.com. Your grid should look like this:

Micro Habit	Read one paragraph	Listen without interrupting	Say no to one request	Drink full glass of water before breakfast	One push-up
Monday					
Tuesday					
Wednesday					
Thursday					
Friday					
Saturday					
Sunday					
Total					

3. **Record your actions.** Every day at the end of the workday, take out your Yes List and simply write Yes or No under each habit. Some days your entry might be an N/A because the opportunity to practice the Micro Habit did not present itself. (Just be on the lookout for using N/A as an excuse!)

Continue with this process for a minimum of four weeks. No increasing yet! After four weeks, if you have more yeses than noes for a Micro Habit, you can then increase the size of that one. Let's revisit Haoyu, whom you met in the Micro Habits tool. After practicing leaving his devices behind for one meeting per day, he slowly increased the number of device-free meetings until, four months later, he no longer used devices in meetings at all. He was able to stop tracking this because the Micro Habit had successfully become a permanent one.

Building on the principles of positive psychology, the log of accomplishments on your Yes List gives you a boost, like earning a little gold star. Your Yes List will help you see where you're making progress toward change. It also gives you a clear picture of where you may be falling short and what you prioritize. I can say I prioritize sleep, but if my Yes List shows I'm netting five hours a night, my results are not in alignment with my goals. A Yes List helps you stay in harmony with the habits you value. Where you're not, you can then recalibrate.

Assessing after four weeks is also a helpful way to notice trends and adjust course early. For instance, to align with her goal of letting go of her propensity for overtalking and eclipsing the voices of her team, my client Liana committed to being no sooner than the third person to speak in one meeting daily (more about this tactic in the Shut-Up Muscle tool on page 105). After a month, we noticed that Liana's Yes List was most sparsely populated on Tuesdays. Curious about what was going on, we analyzed what Mondays looked like for her. It turned out that Monday evenings were jammed. Right after work she refereed her son's soccer games, followed by volunteering at a homeless shelter. As a result, Liana usually got two fewer hours of sleep on Monday nights than any other day of the week. Liana started her Tuesdays with an empty tank, leaving her vulnerable to her default scarcity mindset: *There's not enough time; I need to jump in and solve this, or if I don't speak up, no one else will and we'll waste more time.* Once we discovered this trend, Liana modified her routine on Tuesday mornings by starting meetings an hour later. This allowed her to sleep in and fill her cup—her coffee cup and her mental energy cup—so she could approach her day with a mindset of abundance.

Case Study: Imogen's Story

About seven years ago, my manager informed me there were three direct reports who planned to quit in the next year, and I was the primary reason. This wasn't the first time I had received criticism, but up until then it had always been constructive, with action plans, like "write shorter emails," "practice active listening," or, my favorite, "dumb it down!" Each time I rationalized away their perspective and never committed to any significant change. But this time, I took a very deep breath and accepted my manager's proposal to receive an intense 360 feedback evaluation from about fifteen colleagues of my choosing.

I was devastated reading verbatim comments from my most trusted colleagues who characterized me as inflexible, tone-deaf, with a tendency to overcomplicate and a preoccupation with detail. Reading it stung me to my core. I finally had the appetite to change but didn't know where to start.

I embraced the Yes List exercise and built a spreadsheet to track my behaviors on a daily basis. I had five very specific actions to track, to help me accomplish three goals: (1) be more aware of my impact on others, (2) connect and engage, and (3) coach, don't solve. Creating the spreadsheet was my path to assimilating not just the "how," but the "why" that had been missing from my previous attempts to change. I color-coded the ones I had to "stop doing" as red (such as "don't send instant messages unless it is truly urgent") and the ones I needed to start doing as green (e.g., "when people come to me for an answer, instead of jumping in to solve, pause and ask a coaching question").

At the end of every day, I would review and give myself a "yes," "no," or "N/A." Even now, seven years later, I remember the need for self-honesty. If I logged an N/A or hovered, I realized the only person I was lying to was myself. After a week or two of this awareness, the "noticing in the moment" started happening. I stuck with this for fifteen months.

The end result? I'll never forget what my manager said as I held the doorknob on my way out of the action plan meeting that marked the end of my 360 evaluation. She felt it was "the best investment" she had made. Oh, and the tenure of those three employees? All stayed more than a year after that, and when they did depart, none of them cited my behavior as the cause.

PART THREE

AVOID THE POWER GAPS

Fredrik Backman's novel *Anxious People* mentions a concept that struck a chord for me: rich people buy themselves distance. While we're all familiar with the chasm between the haves and have-nots, the idea of wealth being a physical buffer puts a fine point on the nuances of that division. Earning more money buys you a bigger seat on an airplane with greater space between you and the person next to you, tucked away in a special cordoned-off section; even *more* money buys you a seat on your own plane where you are surrounded by no one but the flight staff. Luxury boxes take the place of sitting knee-to-knee with strangers in outfield seats, public transportation is swapped out for private chauffeured cars, large plots of land put acres between you and your nearest neighbors.

It's much the same with power buying us professional distance. As you know, by its very nature, power creates a natural space between us and those who work for us. On a basic physical level, we move into offices on a higher floor and station assistants as intermediaries between us and others. I've had clients miss the point when they do things like telling their staff, "Trust me, I'm just like you—I have a cubicle instead of a corner office," and then park themselves in a large conference room overlooking the Thames River. Conceptually, we leave the congeniality and familiarity of being just coworkers and get moved to a higher status. When that natural division widens too much, as you now know, it creates the cavernous Power Gaps in which "bad boss" behaviors take root.

Part Three illuminates the three most pervasive Power Gaps that I have seen arise for thousands of managers, and the mistakes each one can unwittingly yield. In each chapter you'll find specific tools for righting those mistakes and collapsing the power distance back to a healthy, productive level.

CHAPTER SIX

The Allure of the Singular Story

In his early thirties, Gerald built a now-legendary gaming program that was purchased for a colossal sum by a venture capital firm. While he could have cashed out entirely at that point, Gerald was still young, brimming with ambition and energy, so he accepted a prestigious offer from another large corporation to come on board as the director of software development. Given this was the first time Gerald had managed anyone other than the two freelance assistants he counted on from time to time, unsurprisingly the transition was less than smooth.

I came into the picture about a year into Gerald's time at the company, at the request of his HR director, because Gerald couldn't keep anyone employed on his team. When he'd first come on board, the younger people at the company were clamoring to work for this demigod of gaming. Within months, the clamoring dwindled as these employees requested transfers to other departments. Gerald's work and reputation were unparalleled, so the company wanted to keep him—but the HR director and his boss wondered, was he really cut out to be a manager?

When I met with Gerald, I was immediately struck first by his roiling frustration. *No one understood him.* My second impression was his ability to command a narrative. Without my even asking, he launched into a rapid-fire blow-by-blow of what he saw was wrong (no one was listening to him), who was to blame (not him), and what needed to happen to enable him to do his job effectively (everyone falling in line to do what he says). This bear of creativity and vision had gotten his paw ensnared in the trap of the Singular Story.

The Singular Story means you're wedded to your version of what's true and right, and that's it. You've assessed the data, concluded how things are and what's needed, and crafted a plan of action. Sounds a lot like effective leadership, doesn't it? But don't be fooled. This is a *"yeah, but"* in action. *Yeah, but I know* the *answer . . . yeah, but I have a proven track record with this . . . yeah, but their ideas and input will only get in the way and slow me down . . . yeah, but this is my vision, my work, my creation—it's good the way it is . . .*

That may all be accurate. What might also be accurate is that like any story, there is no one objective version. There are always multiple perspectives. Often what we consider "facts" or "the truth" are personal interpretations we view through our own lens. Your story of what is so or what should happen may be smart—Nobel Prize–brilliant, even. But could there be more? What if there is an angle you're not seeing, a better version, another more profitable or promising path forward? You know what you know, but what about what you don't know or haven't considered?

My friend Noa told me a story about playing a game called "Salad Bowl" with her wife and four other couples. One person would choose a word out of a bowl filled with folded pieces of paper, each of which had a random word written on it. The chooser would then give their partner verbal cues about the word they'd pulled out so their partner could guess it. The only rule was that you couldn't say the word itself. When it was Noa's turn to choose a paper from the bowl, she gave the clue "Enemy of a canine." Her wife immediately said definitively "Cat!" and made the *nailed it* motion of dropping the mic. Noa said no, that wasn't it, and her wife was laughingly incredulous. "Seriously, Noa, the only enemy of a dog is a cat!"

The answer? Dog catcher. Behold the Singular Story perspective in action.

As the boss, it is certainly within your right to proceed with autonomy. It's not mandatory that you invite in other perspectives, and yours may very well be right. After all, you got where you are because of being right a lot of the time. But a smart boss is not the same as a smart worker. A smart boss has to operate with more intentionality and an eye on the long game. Consider that you're right and able to get the job done by following your Singular Story to its conclusion, but turn off everyone in the process—was it worth it?

"In the beginner's mind there are many possibilities, but in the expert's, there are few," the Zen monk Suzuki Roshi once said. When you stick to your Singular Story, you shut out everything else. The more experienced people become, the higher up they go, the more they become convinced their viewpoint is The Viewpoint. As a result, these experts miss out on the richness and breadth of other ideas that could not only provide an even better solution but also foster more innovation, creativity, and a stronger culture among all team members.

For instance, a common 360 feedback is that the manager very quickly makes up their mind about people. Once they form an opinion—aka their "story"—and write someone off, it's hard to get them to shift. Another common scenario is when managers are locked in battle with each other, hurling accusations based on single assumptions they've each made about the other's motives. The brawl at the top blooms into an all-out battle for their teams. Embroiled in internal skirmishes, they miss opportunities to listen to their team, help customers, and strategically compete in the marketplace.

By asking, "What else could be going on here or what's a different interpretation?" managers and entire teams can save themselves time, hassle, missed opportunities, and frayed relationships, while giving room for ideas, experiences, and people to arise that they may have never expected. Most importantly, they can avoid the Power Gap missteps of shutting out input and mistaking silence for confirmation that their story/plan/solution is the only correct one.

When you signal you aren't interested in your team's input, you widen the Power Gap. This is exacerbated by the fact that those with less power will have a harder time standing up to a boss, especially one who thinks they're always right (remember when Luis needed a microphone but nobody told him so in Chapter One?). When workers feel dismissed and devalued, silent sabotaging behaviors start creeping in. In his book *The No Asshole Rule*, Stanford professor Bob Sutton shares research showing that when bosses discount employees' feelings, employees discount their efforts at work. They deliberately sabotage results, steal from the company, and take more sick days. Fast-forward to a post-pandemic world, and "quiet quitting" is a new term with old symptoms, only magnified several times.

This is precisely what happened with gaming wizard Gerald. If you're wondering why you're delegating and no one is delivering to the level you want, you may have never had their buy-in in the first place. You may think you have everyone in agreement on a strategic plan, but then three meetings later, nothing has moved forward. Many times, when I work with groups, I hear employees complain that their manager hasn't provided a clear North Star. As we unpack the dynamics, we often discover that they were indeed given a clear vision, they just don't agree with the direction their manager chose, so they're either dismissing it, exiting, or staying and silently undermining their boss's efforts.

Mandates without buy-in don't work. As managers the world over discovered in the months following the pandemic, ordering people back in person five days a week backfired. The fulcrum of power has shifted from *positional* to *people*. Workers want flexibility and have the muscle to demand their voices and wishes be heard. Bosses need to be much more aware of how power is used to ensure it's not perceived as a threat, as punitive or coercive. "Because I said so" doesn't work anymore (if it ever did). Succeeding as a boss requires a deep listening to determine how to share power in constructive ways instead of destructive ways, collaborate rather than compete.

Not long after I moved from software program management into executive development at Microsoft, I was put in charge of what was called high-potential development. Every year, the top seven hundred to one thousand people in the company, who had the potential to become corporate vice presidents, would be given development opportunities and direct access to Bill Gates and Steve Ballmer at events, but the program wasn't getting much traction. Coming from engineering, I was new to human resources and didn't really know what I was doing, so that first year I re-created the same blueprint that had been done the year before and quietly wondered when I'd get found out.

It didn't take long. When I rolled out that year's plan, Steve's comment about the plan was, "Sabina, the glass is filling, but it isn't half-full yet." That was his way of letting me know I had a year to turn this around, which I assured him I would.

So I leaned on my old friend, hard work. Ever the engineer, I worked with my team to benchmark and gather data from thirty companies, including GE, Ford, and Boeing, calling each firm's head of learning and development to ask how they identified and nurtured high-potential talent. Out of that I created a new program ready to present at an off-site with all the HR division heads within Microsoft. I figured it would take me three months to implement my revamped program.

I marched into the off-site armed with a binder full of research, ready with my conclusions of what worked, what didn't, and what we should do at Microsoft. Now I just had to report my findings and get their buy-in so I could make good on my promise to Steve and implement this program by the end of the next quarter. Boom, done. My Singular Story was here to save the day.

As I quickly discovered, however, we don't get buy-in without co-creation. These HR professionals certainly didn't want me telling them I knew more about what was good for their employees than they did. I thought I was coming in with an efficient, solid plan, helping them by drafting and iterating it for them and arriving with what I saw as a fully baked program. By minute fifty, not only were they not applauding my efficiency, but they were pushing back hard, saying I didn't understand their people, their history with the company, or the unique needs of their business. I realized that no matter how much data I provided to prove my rightness, it wouldn't fly because it was coming from *me*, and my Singular Story of what we needed to do, and not from *us*. Ten off-sites and six months later, we co-created a program we were all so immensely proud of that quite a few told me they planned to put its invention on their résumé. The end result came from the HR executives *and* me. While we used the research about other companies, we mostly relied on what hadn't worked in the previous program, the wisdom of those who'd had it forced upon them, and our collective creativity.

What was covered in the program remained essentially the same: frameworks and tools on how to be an effective executive at Microsoft. But how we presented the program, communicated to executives and participants, and worked together across the entire company had changed dramatically. Instead of each division hoarding its budget and brewing its version of a program, we had one, well-funded effort. As a result, when a participant moved from one division to another, they didn't have to learn a different set of tools to succeed. I didn't have to spend my time justifying to each division why this was the way to do things; in fact, my HR colleagues backed me up and we all saved time contributing to the participants' learning instead of our internal squabbles. The program ended up lasting for twenty years because it was built with our collective intelligence of what works for high-potential employees in a global organization. For example, in the past, people were nominated in secret, with sometimes neither the employee nor their manager knowing they were on a special watch list. When these employees came to a leadership class, they wondered if they were being sent to "reform school" because they had somehow messed up. We made the program transparent. Now participants came in ready to learn and grow instead of wondering when the other shoe would drop. What's more, those who weren't part of the program had something to aspire to. As the program grew roots, nominees were excited that Microsoft had invested in their development, and they were motivated to remain at the firm.

Ironically, the smarter or more seasoned you are, the more likely you are to get trapped in the Singular Story. High intelligence and a deep well of experience quite often go hand in hand with an impatience for others' ways of thinking. Yes, you need a strong sense of self to stand behind your convictions and not dissolve with every criticism that comes your way. When that sense of self becomes overblown, however, you tilt into arrogance. You lose curiosity and assume that you and only you know the answers. Head down and blinders on, you become ripe to get triggered if someone dares poke at your precious creation. Gerald signaled he was trapped in this righteous mode whenever he interrupted others, before they had a chance to complete a single sentence, with "No, no, no, you're wrong and let me tell you why."

As you peel away the layers of frustration, you usually find an underbelly of fear. Often, people are afraid if they open up to other perspectives, they have to agree with them. This cuts deep to the encoded survival we're wired to protect. If our ideas get mucked with, does not our relevance, our unique position of excellence, wane? If we have to revisit, revise, rethink, doesn't that mean we've failed, not delivered flawless products beyond reproach? Rationally, we know this is ridiculous. Our logical mind knows that opening up to others' ideas gives us greater perspective, out of which we can choose the most viable one. But talk to the survival part of the brain running the show when our singularly sensational story feels under attack, and it's a whole other script.

The quickest way to bypass the Singular Story trap is by employing the Multiple Meanings tool outlined below.

Coaching Consideration: Clues You Are Stuck in a Singular Story

1. **You feel particularly defensive or righteous.** This is often signaled by physical cues, e.g., tightness in your throat or chest, clenched fists, flared nostrils.

2. **You've lost curiosity about others' ideas or perspectives.** Curiosity feels like an open inquiry, whereas a Singular Story holds the sensation of being closed off, impatient, or irritated, wanting and waiting for people to recognize your brilliance.

3. **You're met with silence from your team.** The more strident you are about the correctness of your vision, the less willing your team will be to voice reservations or alternatives. But don't mistake their fear of disagreeing with you for compliance. As the British politician John Morley said of compromise in 1874, "You have not converted a man because you have silenced him."

Multiple Meanings: Rescue Yourself from the Singular Story Trap

Use this tool whenever the following clues of Singular Story appear:

- You are feeling righteous (a mix of frustration and moral indignation at having your viewpoint challenged)
- You are 100 percent convinced "This is how it is/should be"
- You hold a personality assessment of an employee or coworker as fact (*he's sneaky, she's lazy, they only care about themselves*)
- You feel attacked, maligned, or disrespected
- You find yourself stuck in a repeated conflict with a coworker
- You have set opinions about certain colleagues

- You've received feedback from your team that they feel their input is dismissed or devalued

Upon learning what I do for a living, many parents I met when my kids were younger would ask what the most important thing was that they could teach their kids to set them up for future professional success. My answer was the same for success in business as in life, and that was to avoid assuming there is only one way to view a situation.

Knowing this, I created a game with my kids when they were around eight and ten years old to inoculate them against this way of thinking. We called it Multiple Meanings. Every morning, we'd play this game during the time it took us to cross the bridge on the way to school, usually about a minute and a half if the traffic fairies were in a good mood that day. Here's how it worked: one of us would choose something random from the immediate surroundings outside the car, then we'd take turns guessing what might be going on. For example, one time we saw a man walking on the bridge in a sleeveless vest with tattoos covering his arms. My older son, Zaref, said, "His tattoos are fresh, and he needs to wear sleeveless clothes so they can heal." I offered: "He's a lawyer; this is his day off so he can show off his tattoos, which he has to hide at work." My younger son, Ziven, said, "He has a tattoo parlor on the other side of the bridge and is advertising it by showing off his body art." We kept going around until we were on the other side of the bridge.

One day, after a few months of playing Multiple Meanings, Ziven came to me crying. "Zaref is a rat," he shrieked. "He stole my Lego piece!"

I said, "Well, it might be true that Zaref is a rat, but can we play Multiple Meanings and see what else could be going on?"

Ziven sniffled and agreed. Because this game had become so habituated for us, he immediately said, "Well, he could be missing a piece in his airplane Lego kit and saw I wasn't using all my pieces, so he borrowed it." The sniffles stopped as the wheels started turning. "Or maybe he did ask me," he said, "but I had my headphones on and didn't hear him." With each additional story, Ziven's voice got calmer, until he arrived at the conclusion that there were many reasons why Zaref could have taken his piece, and the best way to solve the mystery was to simply ask him. Unhooked from his Singular Story, Ziven was able to let go of his righteousness long enough to learn that Zaref did not, in fact, steal the Lego piece but had seen it under the dresser that morning when he was tying his shoes. No harm, no foul.

In real-life scenarios at work, we swap out Lego pieces for projects and promotions that were "stolen" from us. The rats take the form of anyone and everyone who aggrieves us. And because we cling to our Singular Story, we reinforce our blind spots and seal ourselves off on the far side of the Power Gap, failing to consider Multiple Meanings.

Human beings are storytelling and meaning-making machines. Our species' predilection for storytelling dates back thousands of years. So don't fight human nature. Instead, invite more stories. Because in widening your narratives, you pull yourself out of the Singular Story trap and broaden your aperture into what might be happening or should happen.

Righteousness is a valuable tip-off that you're stuck in a Singular Story. The more you are *absolutely convinced* you're right and are amassing evidence to prove it, the more you would benefit from a healthy dose of multiple storytelling.

Put It into Practice

Step One: Spot the Singular Story

We are usually so deeply enmeshed in our viewpoint that it can be challenging to realize we're stuck in a Singular Story. There are five key tip-offs to look for:

1. You have long explanations for why this is the story
2. You tell a binary story by painting yourself as the hero and the other as the villain

3. When in conflict with someone, you focus on amassing evidence for why you're right (or righteously screwed) rather than asking questions of the other party to understand their point of view better

4. You dismiss the idea of exploring Multiple Meanings as a waste of time (Hello, *"yeah, but"*)

5. No one on your team offers dissent, questions, or other points to consider, and you take that to mean your viewpoint is universally accepted

Step Two: List alternatives

Your next step is to gather more data by considering multiple alternatives. Your process of inquiry follows a straightforward line of questioning: *What else might be possible here?* Or, if this resonates more for you, *What would I say if I were debating this idea from a contrarian point of view?* Keep asking yourself that question until you have a minimum of three alternative stories, or, for all you overachievers out there, until you've exhausted all imagined permutations.

Your answers don't have to be evidence-based; they don't even necessarily have to be probable. They just need to be free of emotional overlay. The answer "Because he's a moron, that's why he did it" is not useful. The aim is to unhook from the fight-or-flight hijack driving you to protect your Singular Story rabidly (and thus your relevance, feeling of control, and dominance).

You don't need to do the Multiple Meanings exercise entirely on your own, by the way. This works even more effectively when we solicit input from others. The trick to gathering neutral data from others is to keep the ask simple and free from your own bias. Use the two magic words I learned from my colleague Mark: "Say more." I use the words "say more" under two conditions: (a) when I'm genuinely curious, and (b) when I'm genuinely judgmental. The opposite of judgment is curiosity. To get out of your judgment brain of what you are convinced is *absolutely so*, stop talking and start asking. This also means asking in as few words as possible. The longer your question, the more likely you are to load it with your own agenda and leading thoughts. So stick with an unembellished "Say more." (And yes, if you and I are talking and you hear me saying, "Say more," you're welcome to ask me if I'm curious or judgy.)

By opening ourselves up to considering not only *one* possibility, but many, we move from a scarcity mindset (one story) to an abundance mindset. This fundamental shift helps carve the neural pathways to train our brains to think like a boss: with plasticity for pivoting and strategy for big-picture imagining.

Multiple Meanings Micro Habits

Once a day, choose a low-stakes situation (i.e., in which you are not emotionally invested) and ask yourself, *What else might be true about why this person did what they did?* or *What else might be going on here other than what I assume?* Make up at least three hypothetical stories in response. By starting with a non-loaded scenario, you build the habit into an ingrained practice so it eventually becomes your default when tensions run higher. (Note: you can choose a situation at work or in your personal life. Many clients have told me this skill has improved the communication in their relationships at home.)

Case Study: Multiple Meanings in Action

Emilio was convinced that one of his new direct reports was slow and lazy. We spent a lot of time each week discussing this guy— let's call him Jeff. Emilio came to one of our sessions particularly aggravated that Jeff had taken three days to finish a report that Emilio believed should have taken only one. The story he told was that Jeff didn't care about efficiency or excellence—a story he backed up with a handful of specific examples to prove to me he was absolutely right.

When I hear someone express that level of crusading to prove their absolute rightness, I know the person has fallen into the trap of the Singular Story. I suggested the Multiple Meanings exercise, which Emilio dismissed as "a colossal waste of time" (another Singular Story tip-off). I then presented him with the Cost vs. Benefit Analysis: What do you stand to lose by entertaining points of view or solutions other than your own? That's easy, we agreed: control. He would have to give up his claim of being singularly right or relinquish autonomy. What he stood to gain, however, was the participation and true buy-in of his team and thus greater productivity. With input from his team, he had a better chance at developing a richer, more accurate conclusion than what he'd come up with on his own. Emilio begrudgingly agreed to do the exercise.

"I'll get us started," I offered. "Maybe Jeff took longer to do that report because he wanted to be extra thorough, knowing how important the information is."

"Okay," Emilio sighed, still not convinced. "Maybe he needed information from others who took time to get it to him."

I countered with, "Perhaps he found a big error and was working all this time to correct it so you and the company didn't look bad."

Emilio nodded and gave a small, "Hmmm." Getting into the spirit now, he suggested, "He might take longer to do things because he gets interrupted a lot by colleagues who need input from him."

The exercise continued for a few rounds until Emilio was noticeably calmer. He was able to let go of his story's narrow singularity and the aggravation that went along with it. As Ziven had done all those years ago, Emilio could approach Jeff in a rational, curious manner. What had taken Jeff so long? Was there something more to the story?

As it turns out, there was. Jeff has dyslexia and takes longer to read through extensive material. Having sensed all along that Emilio was unhappy with his performance, Jeff was additionally worried, further impairing his ability to work expeditiously. Rather than remain locked in conflict and openly frustrated, Emilio devised a plan to give Jeff the time he needed to do the required work. With the metaphorical Lego piece found, the two worked together far more productively. In fact, about six months after this incident, Emilio reported that Jeff had become one of his most trusted people.

CHAPTER SEVEN

Identify Your Communication Fault Lines

I remember the first time I spoke in front of a large crowd. I was twenty-eight years old and had been selected to give a speech to three thousand women at a tech conference. Instead of feeling nervous, I was excited because I'd never been in a roomful of techies with that much estrogen in the air. I confidently strode up to the microphone and started speaking. Instantly, I was startled by how every word echoed off the auditorium's back wall. I continued to deliver the speech at my regular fast pace, but pretty quickly, the echo of the last sentence was blurring into my next sentence, reverberating back to me. I became disoriented and kept losing my train of thought.

I finished the speech and stepped off the stage with much less bravado than I'd felt going on. As I heard the meager applause rather than the thundering standing ovation I'd fantasized about, there was no question in my mind I needed to course correct if I wanted to eventually become an in-demand speaker. I realized my trademark strength of delivering fast-paced energy onstage was the very thing getting in my way when speaking in a larger arena. Bigger rooms and farther-reaching microphones demanded a different pace. In time I learned how to time my sentences, where to pause, and how to attune my cadence so the audience, acoustics, and I were all in sync.

The same thing happens anytime someone ascends to a larger role of authority. Inside the Power Gap, everything sounds different. Maybe not always to your ears, but certainly to those who work for and alongside you. As a person imbued with any level of power, regardless of whether you're the head crossing guard or CEO, you have, in essence, a permanent megaphone attached to your mouth amplifying everything you say. From your side of the megaphone, you may be unaware that your words can hit the ears of those who work for you in ways you don't intend. You may think you're helping when you suggest to a direct report that they work on improving their presentation skills, but to them it sounds less like a benevolent course correction and more like a subtle threat that you're about to knock a few percentage points off their next paycheck. You might think you just pumped everyone up by describing plans to expand your services in the coming year, but your team feels stressed wondering how much more work they were just signed up for. And of course, no one will tell you because it's hard to give honest feedback to people in power.

Because of the megaphone, everything coming out of your mouth is suddenly not only important, but urgent. You email a direct report asking when they can get that report back to you, and they take it as "get this to me ASAP." Your intent may have been simply to know when it was coming back so you could arrange your schedule accordingly or even empower them to give you a realistic deadline that worked for their schedule. Instead, they interpret your mentioning it as a signal that it's a priority they need to jump on right away. They cancel their weekend plans to cram this in, and lo and behold, resentment creeps in.

If you feel a *"yeah, but"* bubbling up here about not having time to walk on eggshells and worry about everyone's feelings because you have a business to run, I'll say this: yes, you do—and a big part of your role in that business is motivating your team and maximizing productivity to achieve the best results.

If there had been only one echo in the auditorium when I was speaking all those years ago, it wouldn't have been a big deal. It was the cascade of echoes that became the insurmountable challenge. In the same way, one communication flub here or there is not a big issue. The real challenge is that when you're the boss, your megaphone is *never* switched off, and over time these little fissures create bigger fault lines. These fault lines, in turn, increase the width of the Power Gap, turning it into a gaping canyon that stands between you and the effectiveness of you and your team getting the job done.

In the thousands of pages of research I've compiled over twenty-five years in my work as an executive coach, the second most commonly cited perceived weakness among managers is poor communication (being hard on others is the first). This offense includes being unclear, inconsistent, overly verbose, not mindful, too formal, not transparent enough, and lacking direction or listening skills. We need to adjust what we say both verbally and nonverbally and—more importantly—how we say it, so that what we intend to convey (or *not* convey) comes through loud and clear.

Much in the same way I had to adjust my speaking cadence in future keynote speeches, when we ascend the career ladder and become responsible for larger teams, we need to shore up our communication. This starts by diagnosing the seven most common communication fault lines that show up consistently in my interview data:

The Seven Communication Fault Lines

1. Uneven Feedback
2. Assuming Cluelessness
3. Verbal Overkill
4. Sage Speak
5. The Past Experience Divide
6. Unspoken Messaging
7. The Uncalibrated Megaphone

Communication Fault Line #1: Uneven Feedback

A key part of Elsa's responsibilities as a director in the nonprofit world was fundraising. She and her small team ran three large events for donors throughout the year. The instant they finished one, work began on the next—that is, after Elsa delivered to each person her morning-after review. A firm believer in growth through feedback, she didn't waste time on what she considered "niceties" and jumped headlong into what her employees did wrong, how they could have handled a situation better, and where she felt they could and should do better for the next event. She would call her direct reports into her office one by one and rattle off a punch list of corrective feedback to each, then launch into her day feeling she had exercised smart management tactics, not just by ticking these three conversations off her list before anyone had even finished their first coffee of the day, but by freeing up her employees to be more productive.

Instead, here's what each of the three people did after receiving their blast of wrongdoings from the boss. Person One searched for jobs online. Person Two griped about Elsa's insensitivity to Person One for an hour. Person Three played revenge video games instead of getting work done. They felt unappreciated, belittled, shamed, and most of all, resentful. After all, they had just completed a major effort, their budget was on track, the donors were gushing. But what did Elsa do? She didn't even say thank you or good job but simply went into "Here's how we can be even better."

Elsa repeatedly fell into the trap of focusing solely on corrective feedback. Giving your employees corrective feedback is of course important and necessary. At the same time, it can't be the *only* feedback you provide. This imbalance is more harmful to their psyches (and hence their productivity) than you might imagine.

Psychologist and relationship expert John Gottman extensively researched what makes a relationship successful. He says that for your partner to believe you have provided them an equal balance of positive and corrective feedback, you need to provide five positives for every one negative comment. Gottman dubbed this the "magic ratio." As human beings, we are wired to listen for the dangers, for the negatives, and don't take in the positive until it's repeated endlessly like this week's top song.

If you're thinking, *Okay, sure, but that's love; this is business*, let me reiterate: all business interactions are personal. We're all human; we don't leave our human psychological makeup at the door when we start work every morning. And let me assure you, beyond the human emotion aspect of feeling unappreciated, there's a business impact to your skipping positive feedback, in the form of lost productivity—not to mention how well your people rate your effectiveness as a manager.

In a survey of more than seven thousand managers, leadership development consultants Zenger Folkman found that 37 percent avoided providing positive feedback. This is backed up by my conversation with clients. They laugh nervously or raise their eyebrows when I mention the "magic ratio," arguing that they either don't want their employees to feel they can now just rest on their laurels or that they don't have time for "coddling." But the laughter subsides and the eyebrows fall when I tell them research shows that people receiving positive feedback net 12.5 percent greater productivity, 8.9 percent greater profitability, and have a 14.9 percent lower attrition rate. Zenger Folkman found that a whopping 69 percent of employees said recognition of their efforts would lead them to work harder.

Let's also sift out praise from positive feedback. Praise is saying, "Good job." While it can be helpful to know someone saw you and appreciated you, at times it can also feel patronizing. And, like demolishing a cookie in two bites, its effect is fleeting. Pretty soon you're craving another one—whether that's an almond cookie (my favorite) or an atta girl. Neuroscience has proven that being praised triggers the feel-good chemical dopamine in the brain, and who doesn't want more and more of that? Our attention naturally then goes to performing for the praise rather than for the result.

Positive feedback, on the other hand, doesn't just skim the surface like praise. While it does trigger a dopamine hit that has been proven to contribute to more innovative thinking and creative problem-solving, it's more of a protein-packed meal that can keep you sated for a longer time than empty calories. Praise would be something like "Good job at the webinar today," whereas positive feedback might sound more like "Your webinar was helpful because you didn't just have a framework, you made it come to life through three steps we can immediately apply." Positive feedback couples positive acknowledgment of someone's actions *along with the impact of that action.* The recipient of this feedback understands how they might pair ideas with actionable steps their audience can take right away.

I've been on the receiving end of this kind of feedback and can attest to its staying power. Several years ago, I delivered a two-day workshop on business strategy at a financial services firm in New York. During a break on the first day, a participant named Martin approached me and said, "May I give you some feedback?" I immediately stiffened, thinking, *Oh no . . . what did I do wrong?* I put on my best facilitator face and said, "Sure, that would be great."

"You're very passionate," Martin said.

Silence.

"And . . . ?" I prompted gently, not quite sure what to make of his statement. "Is that a good or bad thing?" I figured he was bold enough to offer me unsolicited feedback, so I could be bold enough to ask for clarification.

"Oh, it's great," Martin replied enthusiastically.

"What makes it great?" I pressed, as much to help him hone his feedback skills as to feed my curiosity about how to engineer excellent presentations.

Martin paused before responding, looking away from me and up to the ceiling and nodding as he worked out how to put words to his thoughts. After a moment or two, he said, "When you varied the tone of your voice and used gestures the way you did, it made me believe in what you were saying because you came across as so enthusiastic. And your animation kept me awake and motivated me to learn."

Nine years later and I'm still recounting this story, having long since forgotten the many "great workshop" compliments I've received from others on their way out the door. After Martin's feedback, I read books and watched videos to learn how some of the best speakers in the world utilize gestures. I hired a presentation coach to give me specific tips on how to best match my words and messages with my body language. Speaking with my hands was second nature to me, but I worked on mastering ways to take it to the next level. To this day, I thank Martin in my head whenever someone thanks me for my passionate speech.

 Pro Tip: Three Ways to Rejigger Your Feedback Ratio

1. **Follow the 5:1 rule.** For every piece of corrective feedback, give five positive ones. When we provide an abundance of well-crafted positive feedback consistently over time, it's much easier for our employees to accept the critical input. They receive the correctives with the understanding you are aiming to further bring out their smarts rather than to make them smart in shame.
2. **Focus on positive feedback rather than praise.** Praise applauds their action, whereas positive feedback also acknowledges the valued *impact* of their action.
3. **Make it a habit.** Every Friday, block out five minutes to review the week. Who deserves positive feedback that you haven't yet shared with them?

Communication Fault Line #2: Assuming Cluelessness

When we know a lot, it can be easy to forget others might, too.

I'd been working with my client Sanjay for about a year when he was invited to teach as a guest professor of economics at a prestigious university. His course was to be a graduate seminar, in which he would teach the twenty-six enrolled students in a combination of lecture and class discussion. At the end of the semester, the students provided anonymous course evaluations. While many of the comments were positive, the same negative piece of feedback showed up repeatedly and needled him, the essence of which said that students felt patronized and talked down to.

"I can't imagine why they feel that way," Sanjay said in our session, clearly perturbed.

I asked Sanjay to send me the evaluations. Pretty quickly, I spotted the miscalculation that irked his students. At the beginning of every class, when he introduced the topic, Sanjay wasted a lot of time giving his students the basics before moving into the more complex material in which he was a renowned expert. The most telltale piece of feedback said, "He seemed to forget that most of us in the class are award-winning scholars ourselves who have been studying the topic for many years."

If this were a gender issue, we might call it "mansplaining," but in the management world, I call it "Assuming Cluelessness." This happens in both talking and listening—talking, as in doing so too much from your perch of expertise before asking what others know, and listening, as in not doing it enough. The latter is fairly common, as the insulated walls of a Power Gap muffle feedback clues. It can be hard to read the room from inside a Power Gap, mainly because you're often met with pleasantly blank poker faces that belie the *Is this person kidding?* simmering underneath.

How will you know? You won't. That's why you have to check yourself.

The two most common scenarios where we forget to ask and listen are when we teach and when we deliver feedback. By "teaching," I don't always mean literally, as in Sanjay's case; I mean any moment when your intention is to coach someone on your team to do something new. Let's say, for instance, that a newer member of your team is going to present to the board. You might start the conversation by prepping them on the roles of the board members, how to comport themselves, how to pace their speech, and so on. All great—but what if that person has been presenting to boards for ten years and you didn't know because you didn't take the time to get to know their experience before launching into your all-knowing expertise? Now you've not only wasted time but wedged some ill will in there. There isn't a person on the planet who doesn't feel annoyed or insulted when they sense they're being talked down to.

Pro Tip: Read the Room

We climb the ladder of success being finely tuned to every twitch of our boss's face, and then when we ascend, we somehow forget to read the faces of those who work for us. One of the easiest ways to avoid the communication fault line of Assuming Cluelessness is to pause and look around the room. Are they looking at you or at each other quizzically? Are they nodding as if in a trance, or are they registering and expressing human reactions to what you're saying? Are they asking questions or sitting silently? Are they making eye contact or scrolling on their phones for Black Friday deals? The clues are there, if you're willing to do minimum detective work.

When delivering tough feedback to someone on your team, it's easy to assume they don't know how well they did or didn't do on that presentation, how their work fell short, or what they could have done better. But there's a more than equal chance that they actually do. Most people are pretty good at knowing when they haven't hit the mark and even better at self-flagellating over their smallest missteps. When you launch right into pointing out their underperformance without giving them the opportunity to share their awareness of how they fell short, you inadvertently add to the sense of shame they likely already feel. Shame is a tough emotion with deep impact on employees' well-being as well as their productivity. Author and professor Brené Brown, who has spent her career researching vulnerability and shame, believes the impact of shame causes us to withdraw and decimates productivity. This is backed up by a 2021 study published in the journal *Frontiers of Psychology*, which showed that when employees feel ashamed, their ability to process and learn from failure is markedly impaired. As a manager who's looking to encourage and coach your team to optimal performance, this makes an excellent case for avoiding the trap of Assuming Cluelessness.

To help with that avoidance, use the Feedback Flip tool below. The Feedback Flip makes delivering critical feedback a productive (and palatable) exercise for both you and your employees. This tool will prevent the misunderstandings and performance-sapping drama that are frequent accompaniments to Assuming Cluelessness.

The Feedback Flip: Delivering Critical Feedback without Drama
Use this tool anytime:

- A member of your team is underperforming
- A star performer gradually becomes unmotivated
- You are unsure how to give critical feedback to someone who works for you without offending or demoralizing them
- You have a need to be liked at all times (which can make delivering critical feedback painful)

The first time I became a manager, I had to give corrective feedback to someone who had been my peer for two years. Elise wasn't producing enough work, and whenever I walked by her office, I noticed she was playing video games. *What the . . . ?*

I lost sleep and drove my husband crazy for weeks by asking repeatedly for advice and role-playing every scenario. When I finally confronted Elise, she said, "I've been waiting for you to have this conversation with me. I know I'm not doing my best work. The truth is I am not really clear on what I'm supposed to be doing, and I've been afraid to admit that to you." If only I'd thought to ask her first. I'm not the first manager to make this mistake.

The word "feedback" makes most of our stomachs churn—both receiving and giving it. Two simple steps make providing feedback a lot easier by flipping what we normally do.

Put It into Practice

Start by asking the person how they think they're doing. By flipping the feedback to start with the recipient, we communicate that we care about their opinion and are hoping to engage in an open dialog, rather than widening the Power Gap by approaching it as a lecture.
For instance, you might say:

- **"I'm curious how you think that meeting went."**
- **"What are your thoughts about how this year has gone for you?"**
- **"On a scale of one to ten, how confident are you about your performance?"**

Unless they're completely cut off from reality, most people have a pretty good idea of how close their efforts come to meeting the mark. I speak at dozens of events throughout the year, often in front of huge audiences, and believe me I know when I've given a kick-ass speech and when I haven't quite wowed the way I wanted to. You'll be surprised in many cases to realize you and your employee are on the same page, and it lifts the burden of you having to spell out every miss.

In the instances when you're not aligned on the level of their performance, it still gives you an entrée into a difficult conversation by first setting expectations that you're not on the same page. For instance, I had another employee who did not deliver to the level I needed for an event, so I began our discussion by asking him to self-assess his contribution.

"On a scale of one to ten, I'm interested to know where you think your participation lands in preparing for the workshop," I asked him.

He nodded thoughtfully and replied, "An eight. I put a lot of time into prepping."

This is someone who had not only made multiple errors in the off-site materials but submitted the workbook too late for those errors to be fixed in time. To my mind, his work rated far less than an eight.

I replied, "Looks like we're not aligned on how you're doing. The good news is, it might just be a matter of what I am (or am not) seeing—and it's still something we need to address because perception is reality."

In a case of nonalignment, one the most powerful words in the English language is "and." For instance, "I see you think you were an eight given the effort you put in, *and* I see that number as lower given the errors which we were unable to correct in time. We're all trying to produce level ten work that everyone feels proud of. How do you think we can do this so our numbers are more aligned?" Remember, as the boss your job is to establish the goal, the outcomes, and the nonnegotiables; the aim of these conversations is to restate those so you're in partnership with your teammate rather than polarized. You may have different perceptions of their performance—*and*, given the overall goal, what can you now create together to meet the shared objective? When you bridge something with "and" rather than "but," you aren't discounting what they are saying or putting your mandate above theirs. You're placing them on equal footing and inviting them into an act of co-creation.

Feedback Flip Micro Habit

When presented with a situation in which you need to provide critical feedback, ask someone their satisfaction level with their work or performance before providing your input. (Note: this might be an exception to the daily requirement of Micro Habits as you may not always encounter opportunities to provide feedback.)

Communication Fault Line #3: Verbal Overkill

Years ago, my husband and I founded and ran an amateur theater company. After several dramas, we were doing our first comedy. Two weeks into rehearsal, our director had urgent surgery for diverticulitis, and we were up a creek. We had six weeks to pull this off, and we were nowhere near ready. My friend Anna, who moonlighted as a director for another troupe, stepped in to assist. Anna was excellent, with an eye for the big picture such as stage placement as well as detail, like when to pause right before a certain sentence for maximum effect. It was exciting to work with Anna. She gave us pages and pages of notes; there was so much to learn and improve.

Then my friend Kyle came in for one rehearsal as a guest director. He had only *one* piece of feedback for us: "This is a comedy, timing is everything. Just speed up your delivery. As one actor is about to say the last word of their dialog, the next actor should start speaking." Kyle's feedback was crystal clear, and pacing was our focus from then on. This play became the best production we did. It felt great to make the audience laugh—something that's harder to do than you might think. After the session with Kyle, I gushed to Anna, "Kyle was great, he only gave us one piece of feedback—to speed things up." Anna's response? "But I told you all that four weeks ago!" Unfortunately, because she had given us *all* the feedback she had, it was hard to know exactly what we should focus on. It's not that her notes didn't improve our performance. The issue was that the avalanche of suggestions had obscured the main point, which made the biggest difference to landing the humor with our audiences.

Our words are already amplified in a management role, so saying a lot has an outsized impact on our audience. This in turn muddles what's truly important.

Your Verbal Overkill as the boss can also stifle other voices that don't have as big a platform. My client Sebastian knows all the answers no matter the topic and is miles ahead of most people in arriving at a conclusion. As the cofounder of a tech start-up with a lot to do and even more to prove, Sebastian thought he was saving everyone on his staff time when he'd interrupt others to cut to the chase. His standard response to others' ideas was "No, no, no . . ." because he'd seen how a similar proposal had failed three years ago or how a competitor had made a comparable misstep. No comment from others, no matter how inconsequential, was left unanswered (at length) by Sebastian.

"No idea is good enough for Sebastian," read one response in his 360. "He wants to win, not just with the competition but with us. He will talk till you drop from exhaustion and say yes to whatever he wants. Sebastian will always interject with his point of view so why bother." Pretty soon fewer interruptions happened in meetings because Sebastian went on increasingly longer monologues. No surprise, Sebastian shared with me in frustration, "Why am I the only one who has these ideas? Why can't others show some initiative?" He could not see how amping up his talking was tamping down the volume from others.

Another 360 respondent commented, "Sebastian sucks at reading the room. He doesn't look up to see if his audience is with him." Sebastian's Verbal Overkill combined with his Singular Story tendencies prevented him from assessing whether others were as impassioned as he was about his message or wishing he would talk less and listen more. Several other comments highlighted Sebastian's habit of over-responding—to Every. Single. Thing. Often when somebody's brain works really, really, *really* fast, and they feel like they must comment on every conversation, it has the opposite effect of what they hope. It bogs down communication as their message gets diluted amid the stream of words.

Like Sebastian, a lot of my clients are described in their 360s as "forces of nature." They make things happen by flexing their muscles and applying formidable brainpower. This is both useful and, at times, counterproductive. When running a business, there's a time and place to be the powerhouse who knocks down seemingly impenetrable walls and single-handedly turns the earth on its axis. That time and place is *not* when you are wearing your manager hat.

Being the boss means moving into a more subtle art. If you continue to flex your well-toned biceps, you set up a polarizing dynamic in which you're the superhero and your team the supposed underlings to be saved. As you know, swooping in with answers, commanding the narrative, and filling the space with your expertise do little other than feed your hunger to be needed or prove you're the best. Once you've made it, you don't need to keep proving your competence. Your power now will grow stronger through your ability to read the room, pay attention to how others interact, and create space for others to grow strong. The main muscle you need to build now to counteract Verbal Overkill is the one I call the Shut-Up Muscle.

The Shut-Up Muscle Tool: Exercise the Power of Staying Quiet

This is a particularly useful tool to use anytime you notice:

- You are not getting quality input from your team
- You find you consistently have to provide answers or ideas
- You are starved for time and mired in minutiae

The Shut-Up Muscle gets exercised through two related but distinct actions: waiting to speak and not interrupting. In either scenario, you relinquish absolute control over the narrative. You don't necessarily have to give up being the smartest person in the room, but you do give up the opportunity to broadcast and prove that point over and over. Your hunger to be needed or to be the best doesn't get sated the instant it starts grumbling.

That's a lot to lose for some of us. So what do you stand to gain? The chance to be the kind of boss who inspires and nurtures brilliance on your team. By shutting your mouth and inviting players onto the field, you collapse the power distance and create an atmosphere where your team members feel heard and well coached. At the same time, you benefit from the richness of their unique contributions, and who knows, they might come up with even better ideas than you had—or together, you might achieve what you couldn't have done on your own.

Put It into Practice

You can exercise your Shut-Up Muscle several ways. If you tend to be the first person to offer your thoughts, take up outsized space in the room, and/or frequently find yourself impatiently interrupting, try this:

Shut-Up Exercise: Commit to being no sooner than the third person to speak

On the most basic level, not speaking first allows at least two other people to speak before you, even if that means sitting in silence for a few beats.

Being the third person to speak doesn't mean you space out or just bide your time waiting for your turn to talk. What do you do when the first two people are speaking? You listen. Really *listen*. You might learn something, your team will notice and feel heard as you listen and respond to their perspectives, and you can contribute even more thoughtfully and effectively to the conversation.

If a *"yeah, but"* is arising as you read this, about being an excellent multitasker, let me address how you think you can mentally compile your to-do list *and* listen. Research shows unequivocally that we don't fully listen when we're doing something else, and this is when we make mistakes. I see this happen often in group settings when someone who is multitasking is asked a question and has to ask the inquirer to repeat the question.

People mistakenly value multitasking as a virtue. It's held as a symbol of how virile you are in the workplace: *I'm a high-bandwidth person; I can take in a lot; my brain is wired to juggle many things at one time.* Especially now in the virtual workplace, sitting at a desk all day, people insist they have to multitask because they are in back-to-back meetings. Many of us are vulnerable to FOMO (fear of missing out) with emails, even personal ones that rope us in with fake urgency ("25 percent off, today only!").

One way to resist your multitasking desire is to think of one or two questions you might ask about the current speaker's thoughts (while waiting to speak third at least). Not performative questions so you can look smart, but two things about which you are genuinely curious. This also happens to be a great way to make a meeting that you find boring far less so.

People often multitask in the boss's meetings because it's a hub-and-spoke style. In other words, a direct report, or "spoke," speaks only when the "hub"—the boss—asks them to. When someone else is giving their weekly report, seemingly to the boss, why should a peer have to listen? Because if you want your boss's job, you need to be fully present and understand what's going on beyond your silo so you can be more strategic at a higher level. You work in four directions: sideways, up-ward, downward, and outward. A sign you're ready for the next step is that your peers are willing to work for you. The time to work on your peer relationships is now—not to compete with them or try to get them to work for you, but to collaborate and strengthen these connections. Being a boss is about not just how you manage your team, but the footprints you leave and the words that land.

Shut-Up Exercise: Change your definition of "helpful"

We're often quick to jump in when we see someone struggling. This helpfulness, however, is not always the best management strategy, as rescuing can make the other person feel less capable and stymie their growth and development. Executive coach Marshall Goldsmith says we risk displacing a colleague's ownership and commitment by as much as 50 percent when we offer ideas that might improve content by only 5 percent.

Not everything is a problem to solve. We don't always have to jump in and fix a situation right away; we might be doing enough just by listening and engaging in dialog. People are sometimes just looking to be heard and understood, or to run an idea by you as a sounding board.

To ascertain if that's the case and change your definition of helpfulness, pause before jumping in and ask two questions:

1. **What ideas have you considered?**
2. **What would be most helpful for you at this point?**

Asking these two questions enables you to connect with the person you're there to help rather than just jumping in and subsuming their needs with your solution—or hungers.

Shut-Up Exercise: Use Margin Notes

If simply listening can solve so many problems, why is it so hard to do? One reason is that we're worried we'll forget what we want to say if we listen for too long.

Through my work with executive teams, I've developed a simple technique that can help you listen better. I call it Margin Notes. You may already take notes during meetings, but you may still fall into the same trap of interrupting or speaking before you think. Margin Notes allow you to think, process information, make connections between points of discussion, and ask effective questions instead of blurting out the first thing on your mind.

To utilize Margin Notes, set a page with a wide margin (or, if you're using old-school pen and paper, draw a vertical line down the center of the page). In the main body of your notes, capture *only* what the other person is saying. This doesn't have to be verbatim; just jot down key points. If you're using AI notetaking, then Margin Notes might be the only notes you take.

As your ideas, judgments, rebuttals, and questions to each of the points you've written down come up, note them in the margin. By marking them to the side, you separate your own thoughts from what others say. It lets you set aside (literally) your own voice and gives you space to listen to others.

For instance, your Margin Notes might look something like this:

Margin notes	Meeting Discussion
Oliver seems to be more interested in listing all the benefits of X rather than pros and cons.	Need to decide whether we invest further in project X.
Which projects have consistently underperformed?	Decide what we don't do if we move forward with X.
Is Sunita (who's running the meeting) allowing Jack to go on because she wants to gather more data, or is she simply avoiding conflict?	Jack jumps in with the merits of his project.
People are protecting their turf. How can we move them toward a common goal?	Yuval talks about how many cuts his department has made proactively.
People seem to alternate between lobbying for themselves and polling Sunita. They don't talk to each other.	Chris asks Sunita what she thinks.

Shut-Up Exercise: Identify your interruption cues

Do you talk over someone when you think they're wrong? When a joke pops into your head, do you want to blurt it out before the moment passes? Start to track your interruption habits by noticing the cues that pop up right before you act on the impulse. Is it when you feel a prick of impatience, of *Yeah, yeah . . . I got the gist?* Or of irritation when you think they're off track and you have a better solution?

A helpful way to circumvent the interruption impulse is to create a physical reminder of your commitment to exercise your Shut-Up Muscle. Sit on one hand or, if you're in a virtual meeting, put yourself on mute, because by the time you unmute yourself, your impulse will have passed.

 Pro Tip: Two Words to Quash Verbal Overkill

Donna was recapping what she took away from our work together, offering, "I learned two simple words that have been a game changer: 'Thank you.'"

"Say more," I said, using two of my favorite words.

"Well, I have learned that in some meetings when people give me feedback or push back or say things I don't fully agree with or that I want to jump in and defend against or illuminate with more data, it's better to simply say, 'Thank you,'" she said. "It stops me from trying to smother someone with my logic, and I can be efficient instead of being right all the time."

Now that's a powerful and simple way to capture the skill of exercising your Shut-Up Muscle.

Shut-Up Exercise: Paraphrase to stay present

A way to practice presence is to make it about the other person when you speak. Give yourself the task of paraphrasing what the other person has said. You can lead with "So what I hear you saying is . . ." or "Let me repeat what I just heard so I know I'm getting it right." Reflecting comments keeps the focus on the speaker and builds goodwill as they now hear you making a genuine effort to understand their ideas rather than hijacking the conversation. It also helps clear up potential communication issues.

 Pro Tip: Five Good Moments to Exercise Your Shut-Up Muscle

1. When you hear yourself start a story with any version of "Back in my day" or "Where I used to work, we . . ."
2. When you notice any of the tune-out signals in your audience, e.g., checking their phones, too many head nods with no questions or comments.
3. When you have to repeat the same explanation with the same audience.
4. When you catch yourself after interrupting someone. Simply reverse course with "My apologies. I interrupted you. Please continue."
5. When you pose a question in a meeting and no one responds right away.

Paraphrasing can also be helpful when you find yourself repeating what you've just covered because you think someone in the meeting didn't get it. Instead of employing your vocal cords to restate your points, ask someone else to play back what they think they heard. This keeps your word count down and cues others to pay attention because they might need to paraphrase. It shifts you and everyone else to listening and leaning in rather than overexplaining, soapboxing, or talking over each other.

Shut-Up Muscle Micro Habit

Once per day, be the third person to speak, paraphrase what some-one else said, use Margin Notes, or ask a question rather than jump in to solve the problem.

Case Study: The Shut-Up Muscle in Action

Three times a year I run a strategy retreat for a Fortune 50 com-pany. Each time, twelve different vice presidents act as coaches to groups of seven or eight participants, with each group assigned to address a business challenge. I instruct the VPs not to offer any answers. Their job, as I explain it, is to pull their chairs away from the table and observe the dynamics at play. How is the strategy being framed? How is their team arriving at conclusions? How do they get to consensus? The VPs can ask clarifying questions, but nothing beyond that.

At the end of one retreat, one of the VPs—let's call him Andy—was slack-jawed over the breakthrough this exercise inspired. After twenty-five years in business, he realized he had been paying at-tention only to the PowerPoint presentations his team routinely gave, not the process by which they had arrived at their thinking, as he'd done that day. As a result, Andy initiated a wholesale change in how he ran his staff meetings. At the halfway point, he would now pause and check in with the group, asking how they thought the meeting was going on a scale of one to five. Then each person would weigh in from one to five how satisfied they were with their participation, and what it would take to get to a five.

This pause for reflection made his meetings more efficient, opened up communication, and gave everyone ownership of the meeting and its results. Andy realized how often his people would get activated only when the meeting was related to their own work. Now that everyone was on the hook for all of the content, they were fully present. They learned how to work better with each other; for instance, if one person had difficulty getting their voice heard, another would invite that person into the discussion. Communication between the divisions became much more fluid and consensus was far easier to reach in less time.

Communication Fault Line #4: Sage Speak

In *Made to Stick: Why Some Ideas Survive and Others Die,* Chip Heath and Dan Heath write about Stanford student Elizabeth Newton, who ran an experiment in which partners would be paired up, and one would tap out the melody to a well-known song while the other would guess what it was. The tappers way overestimated the percentage of times their tapping would be correctly guessed. While the tappers predicted a 50 percent success rate, listeners guessed only 3 out of the 120 songs, a 2 percent success rate. Welcome to the curse of knowledge.

The curse of knowledge, a term coined in 1989 by economists Colin Camerer, George Loewenstein, and Martin Weber, leads directly to the Communication Faultline I call Sage Speak. When afflicted by the curse of knowledge, we assume that others are on the same level of knowledge and understanding, so we don't bother to explain the core fundamentals (or are frustrated when others don't "get it"). This is especially true with a greater level of experience. If you think this affliction has bypassed you, try teaching the alphabet to a preschooler. We're unconsciously competent at what we can do in our sleep, like our commute; we start and somehow magically arrive at the office the next time we come to. We don't think about it, we don't break it down into component steps, we just do it.

This unconscious competence can become an issue when both experience and seniority are at play. Because we know so much and already think in shorthand, we spout off jargon, especially in TLAs (three-letter acronyms) or speak in broad generalities ("Our purpose is to delight customers"—um, whose isn't?), or give vague, sage on the mountain–style directions ("One and one makes two . . . now go make it happen"). By claiming this hallowed domain of knowledge and hierarchy, we believe we come across even more learned, competent, and exclusive. Instead, we're leaving a wake of muddled, misguided employees who must convene meetings after they meet with the Great One where no one dared to ask for clarification. Instead, the team argues back and forth about who correctly divined what the boss wanted.

Bohdan is a prime example of Sage Speak. "Why is it so hard for them to figure out what's needed?" he blasted. I sat calmly as he continued. "They come to me repeatedly with fresh drafts of the project proposal, and every single time, what I'm looking for just isn't there."

Known the world over for his expertise, Bohdan is far removed from those on his team, who are at earlier points in their careers and don't yet have his depth of knowledge. Bohdan can't communicate what he wants; he can only convulse in anger when he sees what he doesn't want. Moreover, because Bohdan feels pressure to draft his next big speech, he doesn't want to do the work to "get down to their level" to understand their concerns or communicate his ideas. Instead, he spends multiple meetings ranting to the team about how they aren't getting the point. Of course, the quickest way for the team to get the point would be for Bohdan to articulate it.

Bohdan and his team are engaged in what my colleague Liz dubs a "rock-carrying" exercise. The boss barks out an order, "Go fetch me a rock from the parking lot." The team goes out and finds the shiniest, smoothest, largest one. They wash it and prep it and present it to the boss—in a beautiful PowerPoint deck. The boss barks, "This is not the rock I want. Did you not pay attention to anything we talked about? Go fetch me the right rock." Dejected but determined, the team trudges outside and excavates a different rock. Not shiny and smooth but heavy and speckled. They leave the dirt on the rock to give it that distressed look—after all, it matches the cabinet in the boss's office—maybe that's what he wants? This time the boss alternates between barking and begging, "Please spare me! Does nobody here get it? Please find me the right rock this time." The team is now desperate and desolate. Still with no idea about the criteria for a great rock, they're doomed to rinse and repeat until they magically stumble upon the answer, throw a rock through that cabinet, or are tossed out of their jobs.

When we don't pause to make sense to our audience, we create what George Bernard Shaw described as the biggest problem with communication—the illusion that it has taken place.

Breaking the Curse of Knowledge: Margit's Story

As a scientist and clinical practitioner, throughout my schooling and early career I was rewarded for demonstrating mastery of complex ideas. While this served me well in that context, I found I was hitting walls as I progressed to higher-level leadership roles. I would present ideas and plans to others, only to be met with silence or requests for clarification. This would frustrate me and slow down progress.

In talking with Sabina, I began to better understand the importance of shared understanding on a team. Early in my career, I was on teams typically made with others in the same area of expertise. The teams I am now a part of are mostly comprised of those from other disciplines. My value no longer is in exploring the nuance and complexity of my particular expertise, but rather in finding concise ways to summarize my unique perspective for broader organizational success. In order to become the most effective member of my new peer team, I needed to reevaluate the way I communicated.

A key first step was to rewire my ingrained reward system. Demonstrating depth of knowledge was no longer the goal. Rather, my focus shifted to tying my professional satisfaction to team success, which required shared understanding. Seeing the aha moment in others became the reward.

Next, I had to take a hard look at the language and jargon that had been deeply embedded throughout my training. The creation of professional expertise involves learning a new language that admits you into the "club." Club membership is important in some aspects, but also serves as a barrier to entry for others, protecting the domain of the profession. This is a major obstacle to cross-functional team success. I now review every communication to translate information to common language wherever possible.

Communication Fault Line #5:
The Past Experience Divide

Travis was a former member of the US Ski Team with a collection of medals to his name. When he retired from competing, he accepted a job as the head ski instructor at a mountain resort that catered to a high-end clientele. His job was to oversee the team of instructors working one-on-one with ski students. The ski school had been faltering in recent years, and Travis was brought in to make a more cohesive and high-performing team out of the twelve instructors.

Travis came in hot, to say the least. Bolstered by his reputation as an elite winner and certain he knew the right methodology for raising the bar of excellence for his new team, Travis would continually reference his past experience. "Let me show you how we did it when we were training for the Olympics" or "In competitive skiing, we would . . ." was how Travis started his guidance on everything from how to care for the equipment to how to train newer students. His way of leading his new team was to lean heavily on his former successes, which he believed gave him unique insight into how to run the ski school.

On the one hand, your wealth of experience is highly valuable; on the other, no one really wants to hear about it. It's about as appealing as dating someone who won't stop talking about their ex.

Enter the fifth communication fault line: the Past Experience Divide.

People want to know you're willing *first* to take the time to understand them, their environment, and their context. You probably desire the same. Understanding others is a cornerstone of empathy as a leadership skill. Empathy has been shown to increase trust, motivate employees, and improve performance. Research has shown that upward of 74 percent of employees attest they are more effective at their jobs when they think their voices are heard and their values respected.

When you're newly hired or promoted, coming in hot and trotting out your past experience is the kiss of death.

Your team will feel discounted, unseen, unheard. You might have been hired for it, but you can't uniquely claim experience. Each member of your team is also experienced and has wisdom to contribute.

Because Travis was inside a Power Gap, he wasn't attuned to the looks the instructors were giving one another that implied, *There he goes again.*

Travis's actions made perfect sense to him. He intended to bring expertise and excellence to his new role and make the ski resort's instructors as successful as possible. Why waste time inventing strategies from scratch when he already had a medal-winning recipe? Cut, paste, and slap a fresh logo on the formula, and the resort will become another winner.

High-performing candidates in every industry are recruited based on their past performance record, so they naturally come in wanting to prove they were a good hire and apply what made them effective at their previous role to this new one. They want to establish their credibility by securing quick wins. Because they don't have the full context and nuances of their new culture yet, or the internal connections, they have to find some way to offset that lack (and its resulting insecurities). So what do they do? They level the playing field by brandishing their credentials and point to their strong external experience and network. Their words might come from a place of "Look, I know how to tackle this." "Here's what we can do to get us where we want to go," but instead, it comes across as "I've got all the answers, and I don't need to take the time to learn your context or be curious about what you already know." In an instant, they've gone from being the boss offering fresh ideas and a winning perspective to the jerk who has blithely dismissed their team's knowledge and experience. Oops.

Got expertise? Fantastic. Now that you have the upper perch, you'll need to leverage it with equal parts confidence and continued curiosity.

Communication Fault Line #6: Unspoken Messaging

Experts debate the exact percentage of communication that is nonverbal but generally agree it's more than half. Dr. Helen Reiss, associate professor of psychiatry at Harvard Medical School and author of *The Empathy Effect*, developed a training program to allow individuals and organizations to increase their empathetic communication skills. Of the seven facets she identified, five are nonverbal: eye contact, facial expression, posture, affect, and tone of voice (the other two are hearing the whole person and your response to others' feelings). These nonverbal expressions—intended or not—can signal everything from *Wow, you did an incredible job!* to *I am so bored by what you're saying, I want to poke out my eyes with a fork.* The messages you convey without saying a word can reverberate with a force great enough to turn a communication fault line into a full-blown earthquake.

When I run leadership workshops, I do an experiment to prove how deeply people read into the facial expressions of authority figures. Simply by virtue of being the program facilitator, I occupy the authority role in the participants' minds. After we return from lunch on the first day, I take my place at the front of the room (or screen if virtual) and stand there, mute, expressionless, and motionless. At first, there is minor shuffling and slightly confused faces. As the minutes tick by, the shuffling becomes notably more uncomfortable and the confusion morphs into puzzlement, irritation, and exchanges of "What the heck is she doing?" along with looks and shrugs. Still, I just stand there. Eventually, someone breaks the silence and the speculations start pouring out. *Sabina looks irritated with us . . . maybe she is suggesting the workshop isn't going well. She just kind of nodded her head a little, I think . . . maybe she's trying to convey something about us not being good listeners . . . ?*

Then, almost as if on cue, they start to turn on one another in subtle ways. *Maybe she's trying to tell us that the way Lidong challenged her before isn't okay . . . We were all supposed to be in our seats/on-screen and ready at 2 p.m.; I think she's annoyed that only a few of us were . . . Rachel doesn't have her camera turned on, maybe that's the issue?*

Of course, I am thinking none of these things. My point is that because power dynamics run so deep, humans will instinctively read negative cues into a manager's nonverbal communications—even blank ones—as their primordial wiring screams, *The alpha doesn't like you!*

In my experience working with difficult people, most of the negative interactions that spark anger, inspire frustration, and sap employee morale trace back not to spite, power plays, or mind games but simple crossed wires. People take things personally when nothing personal was intended. This doesn't mean that no one is an ass. Just that the roots of most incidents—and their solutions—lie elsewhere.

Consider this scenario:

It's Friday morning and you're headed into work. Jerry, the director of marketing, is waiting for the elevator when you get there.

"Good morning, Jerry," you say. "Any weekend plans?"

Jerry sips his paper cupful of coffee with a stony expression and doesn't respond. *What the . . . ?*

"I'm going to see the new Marvel movie," you add, attempting to break the uncomfortable silence. Jerry squints at you, shrugs, and gets into the elevator without a word. *He definitely heard me that time. What an ass! Is this because I haven't gotten back to him on that email?*

Despite having arrived at work in a good mood, you're now going to spend part of the day stewing over Jerry's slight. You try to focus, but the exchange keeps gnawing at you like an itchy mosquito bite. The more you scratch, the more the irritation grows. *What's wrong with Jerry? In fact, what's wrong with this company? I can't take crap like this anymore.*

I hate to break it to you, but Jerry really doesn't care about your weekend plans. That said, he isn't inwardly seething about that email, either. Nor is he judging you for your entertainment preferences. In fact, he saw the new Marvel movie last week and liked it. The reason Jerry didn't respond when you tried to make polite conversation was that he didn't even process what you were saying. As it turns out, Jerry is not a morning person. He can't be described as completely sentient until after his second venti Americano.

Solipsism colors all our interactions. Being human, we assume that people pay far more attention to us than they do. Without the crucial bit of context about Jerry and caffeine, you can't help but take offense when he doesn't respond courteously. Who wouldn't? If you were aware of Jerry's crippling dependence on caffeine for sustained functioning, however, you wouldn't interpret his standoffishness as anything more than mental fogginess. With a better understanding of Jerry's personality and preferences, you'd correctly interpret his silence as grogginess, not hostility. Or not hostility directed at you; Jerry *may* be the kind of guy who's mad at the sun for rising. Instead of a quixotic attempt at chitchat, you'd give Jerry his space and spend the elevator ride planning the day ahead.

Over time, coworkers learn each other's quirks. Operating in proximity, they can't help but acquire tacit knowledge about each other that softens slights and smooths misunderstandings. Unfortunately, the business world moves so quickly that we're often required to work in high-stakes, high-pressure situations alongside people we don't know well. It's like hurrying to fix something using a power tool without reading the manual: all too easy to get hurt and damage the goods.

Other people would be much easier to navigate if you had a map, a guide to their preferences and pet peeves. Likewise, it's safe to assume that you've been Jerry yourself at some point, unintentionally bruising tender egos and getting in your own way without realizing it. Where's the map for working with you? The Mapping tool outlined below reduces the frustration of crossed signals on both sides.

You are not a morning person, frown when you think, aren't terribly expressive in general—all perfectly fine! You don't have to have a personality transplant; you just need to shift into a productive framework rather than a reductive framework. We want to make your energy, mannerisms, and biorhythm work for you by clarifying to your team how you operate and how best to work with you.

In a Cost vs. Benefit Analysis, revealing your internal map means you stand to lose some of the privacy your elevated perch affords you. Giving up that distance may feel uncomfortable at first. By its very nature, using any tool that collapses distance means you give up a little of your exclusivity and mystique. However, you're helping clarify what's behind the personality expressions your team is already aware of, not revealing deeply held secrets. You stand to gain more trust between you and your team when you share, and to increase the odds for more effective communication. You'll also regain vast amounts of productivity when team members no longer waste valuable time and energy trying to get a read on you. Transparency and better communication lead to trust, which helps dial down your (and their) frustration and amp up your productivity. You create a better understanding, enabling your team to produce improved work and establish a better relationship with you.

Mapping Tool: The Customized Guide for How Best to Work with You

Use Mapping anytime any of these misunderstanding scenarios arise, which are valuable clues you need to bring clarity to your nonverbal communication:

- Others incorrectly interpret your words or demeanor
- You believe your personal boundaries are being encroached upon
- Your expectations are not being met, and you are unsure why
- In response to your unmet expectations, you hear replies that surprise you, such as "I thought that is what you wanted" or "I had the sense that you . . ."
- You hear interpretations about yourself that are not true

Mapping is the most direct route to demystifying the unspoken messaging for those who work for you. It gives your team clear guidelines on how to understand your work style and best engage with you.

Put It into Practice

Mapping is a two-part process. It involves clarifying your personal map coordinates and then charting them for others who may not be able to intuit what's going on inside your head.

Step One: Chart your coordinates

First list the elements that make up your personal map: your rhythms, pace, expressions, mannerisms, learning style, ways of processing timelines, and so on. By their nature, our default settings are not something we spend much time consciously examining. We all assume other people think and act exactly the way we do, until it's conclusively proven otherwise. Instead of leaving people guessing what you want or what you mean and then blaming them when they get it wrong, you'll be able to clearly articulate your nonverbal cues.

To get a sense of what your own norms might be, begin with the following prompts:

- **Physical behavior and demeanor.** How do you tend to carry yourself? Do you wrinkle your nose or close your eyes when you're thinking? Do you sigh often, and what does it mean when you do? Is your resting face more serious than your thoughts usually are, or vice versa? Do you refrain from shaking hands? People from different cultures have different norms about smiling, eye contact, physical distance, and so on. Never assume people know these distinctions. Lay them out.

- **Energy and mood.** Remember Jerry and his coffee? We all have our own rhythms. What are yours? Are you a morning person or a night owl? Think about how your energy and attention fluctuate throughout the day. How might others use that information to get your best efforts?

- **Communication and boundaries.** How do you learn best? Bullet points? Stories? Do personal details feel too intimate, or are you more comfortable with a little casual conversation before getting down to business? What's the best way to reach you in an after-hours emergency, and what qualifies as one? Do you tend to ramble when you're nervous? Should people communicate a clear deadline and let you do your thing, or do you prefer being reminded? What kind of response time should they expect?

- **Personality.** Are you an introvert who needs time alone to process before contributing to a conversation? A detail-oriented person who likes to drill down on facts and numbers before discussing the big picture? A born optimist who winces when people sound defeatist? It's helpful to think of moments of frustration or elation—and what sparked them—as a window into the unique qualities of your personality and style.

- **Thinking and problem-solving.** Some people prefer to be alone to think. Others are more comfortable bouncing their ideas off others. Some like to draw on a whiteboard; others need concrete examples to understand abstract principles. Some plan; others prefer spontaneity. Many procrastinate; many more fiddle with things after they're finished. Where do you fit into the spectrum?

- **Humor.** Are you comfortable with jokes and wisecracks? Do you occasionally lean a little hard into sarcasm? Do you believe there's a wrong time for humor?

Pro Tip: Solicit Input on Your Coordinates

To gain greater understanding of your personal operating system and nonverbal quirks, and rhythms you may not be aware of, ask your friends and family for their input. Who better to reflect these insights to you than those who know your shoes-off self?

Step Two: Map your terrain for others

Step Two translates those elements into a usable map to help your team navigate how you work. Our habitual ways of thinking and doing may seem obvious to us, but they're often anything but that to others. In my experience, an enormous amount of tension evaporates when the implicit is made explicit.

Once you've completed the list of your norms, create a second column that lists what you will do to communicate each of the personality elements you noted. This gives both you and your team specific instructions for heading off conflicts before they happen. Many if not most of the common quirks you'll identify are addressed in this book, so read through it again with an eye toward simple fixes for this second column.

For instance, your map might look something like this:

Personal Coordinate	Effect/Action:
I frown when I'm thinking.	When someone pitches me an idea or discusses an issue I need to consider, I let them know I frown so they do not misinterpret it as disdain or dismissiveness. If I need to deliberate, I will acknowledge the other person's contribution first: "You've made an important point. Let me think . . ."
I lose steam (and/or patience) by late afternoon.	I will let my team know I would prefer to schedule important meetings earlier in the day, when I concentrate best.
I do not like to multitask.	I will let my team know if I send their call to voicemail not to take it personally; it means I was concentrating on something else and will call them as soon as I can fully focus on their needs.
I do my best work late at night, so it's when I tend to send a lot of emails.	I notice how my preference creates angst because my team feels they need to respond or be reachable during those off-hours. To mitigate this, without having to change my personal biorhythm, I will set up a delay in my email server so the messages go out the next morning.
It's hard for me to pay attention if I don't know what you want from the beginning.	I look annoyed in those instances, because I am. To prevent this, I will say, "Can we please pause for a moment, and could you give me the upshot of what you're hoping to accomplish in this discussion? It would be helpful for me to know at the outset so I can listen with that in mind."

There is no ultimate right or wrong way to be in these categories. Your only goal in mapping is to avoid unintentional communication fault lines. Getting clear on your tendencies and helping the people around you get a better idea with whom they're dealing is a far more effective approach to working together than trying to change yourself, or, worse, trying to change someone else.

Mapping in Action: Giuseppe's Story

As a new leader in a new institution, I had a lot to learn. My manager suggested I spend time building my leadership team, and I changed the leadership structure to better meet our needs. As a result, almost the entire management team was new to their positions, some in leadership positions for the first time. As we started working together, it became clear that each of us had our own communication style. The challenge was to get us all working together as a team toward shared goals and find the most efficient ways to communicate with one another.

One of the challenges I encountered was when leaders would bring up controversial topics in large group meetings instead of giving me a heads-up first. Others were still feeling out the scope of their position, leading to some boundary conflicts. It felt like now was a good time to bring the team together in an off-site. Sabina and I worked together to design a program to build harmony, bonding, and trust among team members.

We used the Mapping tool as a way to discuss personal preferences for work style, mine included. As each member presented their working style to the group, there were a lot of head nods of *ahhh, now that makes sense!* We found out who can't follow long emails, who prefers a quick call or text, and who needs all the background info about a project. We saw who is really stressed outside work for time and attention, who is hands-off, and who needs more face time. Mostly, we all got to know each other better and deeper.

The tool gave our team a way to open up and communicate working styles and preferences with each other. Most of us didn't even realize the different ways that people work, which may not be the same as our own. Two years later, our team is working very well together. There is a lot of cross talk, collaboration, and idea-generation. Although the team still has some communication issues now and then, we now have a common understanding and shared language to discuss concerns as they come up. Our leadership team is maturing and gelling for the good of the organization.

 Mapping Micro Habits

- Once a day, explicitly make the connection between a nonverbal signal and your intention. For example, "I'm looking down while we're on this video call to take notes," or "Frowning is my thinking face, and you've given me good fodder for thought."
- Ask someone else to clarify their map. "I notice you've been frowning. Is there something I can clarify?"

Communication Fault Line #7: The Uncalibrated Megaphone

As you already know, as the boss, every toss-off comment you make carries weight. Your maybe becomes a definite. "I like where this is going" becomes "It's greenlit." An innocent question of "Why did you think of it this way?" causes your team to think they need to completely revamp their approach.

Sometimes, a disconnect between message intent and reception points directly to the communication fault line I call the Uncalibrated Megaphone, in which your words are being received with more (or less) volume than you may intend. This can confuse your employees, spiking anxiety and impairing their ability to do optimal work. Given that your new definition of success is to empower *their* success, you can see why appropriate volume modulation is so crucial for everyone in the mix.

Take what happened with Mei, for instance. Mei's stomach churned all night after her manager Tuan had told her, "You could have a bigger impact." A week of nail-biting anxiety and difficulty focusing followed, in which Mei wondered if the comment was a veiled hint that her job was in jeopardy. Finally, Mei scheduled a one-on-one with Tuan to ask for more clarification.

"Did you mean five percent more impact or ninety?" Mei asked to kick off the conversation.

As Mei relayed to me after, Tuan looked taken aback. He had no idea his comment—which he clarified as closer to a 5 percent suggestion, enough to give Mei a boost and garner her greater visibility and a future promotion—had landed with 90 percent force and caused such distress. He quickly assured her, "You're doing a great job, Mei. You're a strategic thinker, and I want you to consider additional projects where you can apply your strategic thinking strength to have an even bigger impact on our bottom line."

Because of the complexities buried in power dynamics and our human wiring around authority, your team is primed to hear more negatives than positives, take things personally, and make the proverbial mountain out of a molehill. If Tuan had simply said, "On a scale of one to ten, you're a ten, now let's figure out how to get you to an eleven and boost your impact and visibility," his intentions would not have backfired. Mei could have spent an entire week directing her energy to working on her path to eleven instead of losing focus and productivity thanks to an amygdala hijack of worry and shame.

You may be unaware of how your micro actions have macro impact. When you're busy, you might not realize you're being vague when it comes to giving directives or feedback, creating crossed signals and loss of productivity. The Scaling tool explained below eradicates these issues, quickly and powerfully.

Scaling: Landing Your Words with Intention

Use Scaling anytime one or more of these scenarios arise, signaling you may be vulnerable to the Uncalibrated Megaphone fault line:

- **Conflicts and misunderstandings are arising between you and those who work for you**

- Members of your team are not following your directives
- You are not confident your team understands the impact of something (e.g., they are not giving it the appropriate emphasis and time)
- Your expectations are not being met

The Scaling tool, which was shared with me several years ago by a colleague, enables you to calibrate what you say and how you communicate so what you say lands with the impact or level of urgency you intend.

Scaling, as an action, means being targeted and specific in your comments and then sharing the amplitude of your feelings. By giving your reactions or requests appropriate context and weight, you reduce the possibility of misunderstanding. You also let your teammates in on your thought process. Rather than leaving your employees wondering what you meant or what you're thinking, you approach these exchanges more intentionally. In return, your team feels valued rather than defeated.

The thirty seconds it takes to clarify for your employees how your comment rates on a scale reduces the chances of misunderstandings and yields an exponentially greater return in their productivity.

Put It into Practice

Scaling uses a simple one-to-ten rating system to put a comment, request, or feedback into context. Here are four ways to apply this system:

1. **Urgency or importance of a task.** That might look something like:
   1. On a scale of one to ten, I'd rate the importance of this task at a ____.
   2. This is a __ on the urgency scale. Are you able to get this back to me by (date/time)? Or, by when can you get it back to me? (see #4 below for follow-up)
   3. In terms of rough sketch vs. polished, this can be a ____.

2. **How strongly you feel about something.** This could include:
    1. On a scale of one to ten, I consider this issue a ___.
    2. My excitement/concern level over this is a ____.
    3. The certainty/hesitation you're hearing in my voice may not accurately reflect my feelings; I'm actually at around a ___ on this issue.

3. **The degree to which you appreciate or want someone to adjust their effort.** When giving feedback, specify:
    1. On a scale of one to ten, your value to the team and/or me is at level ___.
    2. I'd rate my concern about your performance at a ____.
    3. You are already at a ___; I'd like to see you get to a ___.

4. **To gain an understanding of how others feel by asking *them* to scale.** For instance:
    1. On a scale of one to ten, how confident do you feel about your ability to deliver in the timeline I've given?
    2. To what degree do you agree with my assessment of your performance?
    3. How clear are you on the direction I've shared?

Essential to the success of this tool is that you're consistent in your rating system. If you rated the importance of a task as a seven, make a note of what it entailed. What were your expectations around a seven? The more consistent you are with your rating, the quicker your team will understand fully what you mean and expect with each scaled number.

And watch out if you're rating everything too high or too low. If you're charging from task to task in a hurry, for instance, you may be on overdrive and mindlessly rate everything a ten on the urgency scale. If you're a caretaker by nature (more on that in Chapter Eleven), you may by default underrate the importance of tasks, not wanting to overload your team. A hunger to be liked can tempt you to downplay the level of critical feedback because you don't want to hurt someone's feelings. You get the picture. Bottom line: vet your number choice as objectively as you can.

Scaling Micro Habits

- Once a day, instead of providing a binary answer ("That's great" or "This needs work"), specify your response on the scaling spectrum ("On a scale of one to ten, this is a nine" or "This is a five and needs work in X area to get it to a seven").
- Ask a question using Scaling. On a scale of one to five, how important is this to you? Or on the spectrum from don't care to this is really important, where would you place yourself?

Communication Fault Lines Mended: Vera's Story

I am a firm believer in brainstorming and discussing different points of view to reach the best conclusion. My approach used to be to get together with my team and actively comment on issues they were bringing up, offering my point of view and the challenges I saw to their suggestions. People who had been working with me for a while or who knew me well understood I was open to being challenged and willing to change my opinion if they offered a better idea. New or not-as-outspoken team members saw me as authoritative, telling them what to do, and micromanaging.

Through coaching, I changed my approach. I now arrive at these meetings with an open mind and without predefined ideas. I make sure I am at least third to speak. To manage my anxiety (since sometimes I reach a conclusion while others are still processing the issue), I write margin notes, along with notes on good points that other team members are making. When I am ready to speak, I start by paraphrasing some of the things I wrote down, for example "John, I think your idea of ____ is excellent," and then I move on to asking open-ended questions, like "What are your thoughts on . . . ?"

or "How would you . . . ?" while calling out everyone in the room to ensure they participate.

I have come to understand that if you are the most senior person in the room, whatever you say will be considered a must-do instead of just another opinion. So I use my revised approach to guide the team but allow them to bring their A game, feel listened to, and most importantly, to know the decision on the approach came from them, making them more accountable and committed to the task ahead.

CHAPTER EIGHT

Dispel the Myth
of the Exceptional

By age twenty-eight, Alex had generated more revenue and critical acclaim for the film company he worked for than any executive in the firm's history. Given his hotshot status, people in the office were willing to put up with his odd personal quirks. And by "odd," I mean obnoxious. Each morning Alex would pluck the daily periodicals off his assistant's desk and disappear into the bathroom for half an hour. On his way out, he would casually slap the papers back down on the assistant's desk, oblivious that those pages were now considered soiled. Alex also had a distasteful habit of immersing his fingers into whatever he ate, from French fries to chicken breasts. He'd then lick off the sauce, and if someone came into his office, he'd shake their hand.

As time went by and Alex brought in and earned more and more money, his quirks magnified. Throwing his weight around at restaurants to get the best table, showing up for meetings unshowered, and dismissing input from colleagues as "stupid" were just a few of his idiosyncrasies.

So what happened here? Like many high-status achievers, Alex conflated *excellent* with *exceptional*.

Excellent is producing great work, something Alex absolutely did. Exceptional, however, is believing the rules don't apply to you. In Alex's case, it was the rules of basic hygiene and civility. Other bosses who think they're exceptional and buy into their own mythology become headlines of embezzlement, interpersonal misconduct, ultimatums, red-faced rants, or worse. I won't regale you with horror stories here; just search "CEOs behaving badly," and you'll quickly come across dozens of examples. I lost track of Alex not long after this phase of his career, but given that these behaviors usually start small and rapidly spiral into larger crimes and misdemeanors, I would not be surprised to one day read about Alex being in serious hot water.

At the core of exceptionalism is a sense of entitlement. I don't mean a Veruca Salt from *Charlie and the Chocolate Factory*, foot-stomping, spoiled sort of entitlement (though in some cases it is), but rather a sense of having earned certain privileges. Ascending to the next level in any position requires a certain amount of sacrifice and accommodation. There isn't a single client I've had in the twenty-five-plus years I've been an executive coach who doesn't have a list of Little League games or gymnastics meets they missed, vacations that got cut short to deal with an emergency, or hours of sleep they've given up for important projects. Certainly, financial rewards go a long way toward compensating for these sacrifices, but do they go all the way? Not usually, and I'll explain how the whole system silently spins on that axis of deservedness in a moment. Like an emotional petri dish, the difference between what we're paid and feel we deserve for our sacrifices is a ripe catchall for entitlement to breed.

It's easy to lose your footing inside the Power Gap when the walls are padded with praise and goodies. The cult of celebrity that gets created around those in high positions practically tells them they are entitled. *Here, you're amazing . . . have some cookies!* Their moral compass gets skewed as they reach for more and more. And of course, because of their status, no one calls them out on grabbing more cookies than they're entitled to, until it's too late. Even if someone did, the boss would probably have already teetered into *"yeah, but"* territory and would dismiss it.

The cookie-grabbing, so to speak, usually starts small. A slightly nicer restaurant or an extra glass of wine that goes on the expense report after nailing a project "because I earned it" and "I deserve a break and something nice for myself." This makes sense because as our responsibilities increase, so do the pressures on us. As we ascend, work requires more sacrifices. At some point we want to even the scales, and that extra glass of wine on the company expense report becomes extra nights at a fancy hotel after the out-of-town conference is over, even though it's a poor substitute for not being home for our partner's birthday last month.

What makes exceptionalism more complicated is that others encourage and support our elevation to special status, as they ply us with ever more extraordinary rewards the higher we go. We receive the office on the top floor with a better view, the exclusive club membership where we can meet high-flying clients, a big salary bump or an elaborate bonus structure, and so on. Ensconced in our bubble of special, we relax into our status. The Power Gap widens as the voices of those who would catch us early in our missteps get muted, and—well, you know what happens from there.

Personally, I believe it's important to enjoy the fruits of your labor. Otherwise why are you working so hard? But I differentiate between enjoying the fruits you've grown and those you start taking from other people's trees.

Organizational psychologist Merete Wedell-Wedellsborg says three things can feed unethical behaviors:

1. **Omnipotence:** the boss believes they are more powerful than anyone or anything (including the rules).
2. **Cultural numbness:** teams become inured to the manager's behavior because it has slowly crept up from slightly odd to quite inappropriate (think: hotshot Alex).
3. **Justified neglect:** teams indulge in self-protection. After all, who wants their paycheck docked for pointing out a boss's padded expense report?

I'm in no way suggesting that the manager crossing these lines is innocent, but notice the entire system around them is complicit. As Harvard professors Ronald Heifetz and Marty Linsky say, there's no such thing as a dysfunctional system. It exists because it serves everyone in it—in one way or another—otherwise it would have changed.

How is the whole system complicit? As long as the boss delivers high-yield results, others are willing to look the other way when that person makes tone-deaf jokes or berates their assistant because the coffee isn't hot enough. Their higher-ups might send them to "charm school" by enrolling them in an executive education program or having them work with a communication expert and hope the problem will go away. Or, at the very least, they can show they took steps to mitigate it.

Many corporations see the shiny outer layers—the key results—and don't want to confront the truth behind them. There are plenty of yes-people who also insulate high-performing bosses from the truth tellers. As a result, that individual falls into a good/bad binary mode of thinking. No one calls them out on their behavior and everyone calls them a good leader, which they take to mean they can get away with anything, saying whatever and operating as they please. It's easy to confuse being the superior (a noun) with being superior (an adjective). They start to believe their own PR, that they're above others, that they're untouchable.

In other words, they buy into whatever *"yeah, but"* is justifying their behavior.

It takes courage and a healthy dose of humility to be willing to see or admit that you're on the cusp of this gap or have already fallen in. The biggest clue is if you find yourself saying things like:

- *"I've worked hard, I deserve this."*
- *"So-and-so at the top does it, so I can do it, too."*
- *"I don't have time to (track down all the receipts for my trip . . .*

worry about what people think . . . add in all the niceties . . . wait in line)."

- *"I've sacrificed going to all my son's soccer games, the company owes me."*
- *"No one around here has done as much for this company as I have."*

These beliefs fuel Myth of the Exceptional behaviors, which trickle down beyond one offense, creating a toxic workplace. Berating your assistant in front of everyone for forgetting to get mayo on your sandwich isn't just bad for their self-esteem; it shows others how you might treat them. No one wants to work in a toxic work environment. It also robs the team of productivity because people focus on injured feelings and self-protection instead of doing quality work.

While your abilities may be excellent, none of us is entitled to ignore the basic rules of civility and ethics. You can be the best and still steer clear of "exceptional" and all the intoxicating blindness it entails. Because no one will likely tell you before it's too late, it's up to you to keep yourself in check. However, you can use the Solicit Feedback tool below to increase your chances of avoiding being seduced into this myth by recruiting help from others.

Pro Tip: Good Intentions Don't Count

Too often I hear badly behaved bosses repeatedly assure me they have good intentions. But intentions don't matter. Actions do. As a manager, let's just assume you have good intentions. As I tell my clients, better to keep that verbal declaration of benevolence to yourself and *show* us your intentions instead. Just like our values are evident by how we fill our calendars, our assurances are only as good as our actions.

Solicit Feedback: What Do You Need to Do More or Less of?

Use this tool anytime:

- **Something isn't going quite right between you and those who work for you, but you're unsure what it is**
- **You are getting a lack of input or pushback from your team on your ideas**
- **You have a revolving door of problems and questions from others**
- **You are unclear what you could be doing differently or better to improve performance**

The best way to shed light on where you might be veering into problematic territory is to ask those who work for you. But thanks to the Power Gap and the reluctance of most to risk speaking truth to power, it's not quite as straightforward as just poking your head into someone's office and inquiring, "What do you think of me and my management style?" Yikes.

As the boss, asking for "open feedback" doesn't even come close to a real invitation, because the only answers you'll get are "you're doing great" or straight-up crickets chirping. As you'll read more about in Chapter Ten, we can thank our hidden unmet hungers for that (well, hidden to us, at least). When people give feedback upward, they're so finely tuned into our hunger signals that they will feed them and provide nothing more. My client Quin, for instance, had such a need for praise that her people doled it out to please her. As a result, she received no meaningful feedback on what was impairing her performance. Hello, blind spot.

Soliciting feedback is a potent means to illuminate your own blind spots and collapse Power Gaps. This smaller gap that creates more connection with your team is the gain in the Cost vs. Benefit Analysis. But the work does not end there. The ask is only half a tool. The other half speaks to what you will do with that feedback. Will you let in critical feedback and be willing to step outside your protective walls of blissful ignorance?

Receiving honest feedback means allowing yourself to be vulnerable. It requires serious leveling up of your willingness to admit your own weak spots and grow. That is a cornerstone of success at the highest levels, as it shapes your ability to think strategically in new terrain. A Korn Ferry study showed that professionals who remained curious, open-minded, and willing to admit when they'd gone down the wrong road were the most effective in the face of new and unfamiliar challenges. Executives who displayed this willingness to be agile were also shown to produce 25 percent higher profit margins.

Put It into Practice

This tool has two parts. The first is making the ask for feedback using one of the approaches below. The second part—letting in the feedback—is an internal mindset shift we need to make if we are serious about taking charge of our effectiveness.

Part One: Make the Ask

Any of these three approaches will arm you with the tactical finesse to solicit helpful feedback.

Approach #1: Ask for Specifics

The quality of the feedback you receive is directly proportional to the quality of your request for it. Instead of vague generalities that will encourage your team to tell you more of what they think you want to hear, drill down and ask for specifics. For instance, instead of "How did I do?" ask, "What's one thing if I did more or less of it, it would make your life easier?" An ask for "one thing" gives a straightforward and simple directive. Don't go too far with this; "What's my one weakness?" is way too scary. Instead, opt for "What's the one thing that would make me more effective? What's one thing if I did more or less of it, it would make *you* more effective?"

What you don't want to do is put your employee on the spot. Blindsiding them invites everything from uncomfortable (and useless) platitudes to a full-on amygdala hijack for them as they freeze and fumble for what they think will please you. Even the most considerate, articulate person needs time to consider an ask like this. You can pose the question ahead of a scheduled meeting and then have the discussion. Or you can ask the question directly in a one-on-one meeting and let the employee know they can respond when you next talk. Over time, you can ritualize this, letting them know you will ask them this in your one-on-ones so they're prepared—and it becomes no big deal.

Approach #2: Use Scaling

As you learned in the Scaling tool (page 127), it's often easier for someone to pin feedback to a number. You can ask them to rate your management performance (either in general or on a specific project) on a scale of one to ten. If they rate your management performance at say a seven out of ten, you can then follow up by asking, "What would it take for me to move from a seven to an eight?"

Approach #3: Externalize the Ask

If you're sensing hesitation on your teammates' part to be transparent, try externalizing the feedback. For instance, you might ask, "What would someone who was super critical say?" That way they don't have to own it and can say it on behalf of nameless, faceless others.

Part Two: Take in the Feedback

Now comes the hard part: you need to listen to their responses. Really *listen*. As my colleague Mark Yeoell says, the quality of someone's speaking matches the quality of the listener's presence. If you want quality feedback, you need to bring quality presence.

If I had to point to one trait that every successful CEO I've worked with has in common, it is that they are fully present. Beyond their engaged body language and eye contact, you can feel it in the quality of their questions, their responses, the playback to what they're hearing, and their interpretation of what you're saying.

Bill Gates was a perfect example of this. He would listen intently and then ask questions that one could ask only if they were fully present. He was famous for burrowing into an issue to understand the topic deeply, not just at a surface level.

Everyone wants the fast pass, but the answer lies in you being present. All you have to do is show up and listen. It's that simple, and that difficult. Full presence means no devices, no multitasking, full eye contact, and—when appropriate—paraphrasing what you heard or asking follow-up questions to dive deeply into what they're saying.

This full presence gives you the insight you seek. But it also reaches across the Power Gap to put you in collaboration mode with your teammates as the boss who will bring out the best in them.

 Solicit Feedback Micro Habits

- Pause after you've spoken or interacted with someone and ask yourself, *What's one piece of feedback they would give me about that interaction?*
- Take stock of your day and give yourself feedback. *What's one thing I did well? What's one thing I could have done to make the day go even better?*

PART FOUR

NAVIGATE THE HIDDEN PRESSURE PITFALLS

"I'm in deep shit."

From the tone in Benita's voice, I knew it was serious.

Fierce and admittedly intense, Benita practically vibrated with powerhouse energy. When we'd met at an event two years prior, she was a lobbyist, known in her industry as a tiger who made the impossible happen. In typical strategic Benita fashion, she tucked away my information into her coveted contact list in case she ever needed me. Three months into becoming the first woman president of a nationally lauded nonprofit, she called me in a panic.

"The entire staff is threatening to stage a walkout, they hate me so much," she said. "I have no idea what I'm doing wrong."

The board loved her, which is why they wanted to invest effort into getting Benita back on track, not to mention the terrible PR if she left after only three months. The organization brought me in to observe Benita, conduct a 360 review, and deliver the feedback to her. Over the course of two days, I interviewed everyone in Benita's immediate domain, from all directions—direct reports, board members, and a wide range of staff members. The last night, I had dinner with Benita to discuss the results.

On the plus side, I told her, she was unilaterally considered a dynamo. Her team and the higher-ups had noticed and appreciated how she mobilized her trademark vision and employed tenacity to change internal systems in three months that would have taken mere mortals three years. Tapping new funding streams through her vast array of contacts, she was on her way to multiplying the organization's bottom line. On the other hand, what also surfaced were pages and pages of searing commentary about how Benita shut people down, lost her temper, had zero empathy, and clung to her singular ideas of what she wanted to do and how she wanted to do it. The animosity was palpable. Benita was right—she *was* in deep shit.

A large number of people I work with fall into this category. Either they don't know what's standing in their way of being a successful manager, or they know it on a superficial level but don't understand the intensity of it or the level of its impact. They have no idea how poorly they're coming across. They'll shrug and say to me something like "Yeah, I know I'm impatient, or aggressive, or not the best listener . . . ," but they have no idea that people are throwing up in the bathroom out of fear before meeting with them. All they know is that they're aggravated by their team's lack of skill or dedication or demoralized because being the boss is nowhere near as fulfilling as they once imagined it would be. Either way, they don't see under the covers to the deeper psychological reasons why any of this is happening.

The answer, as we've already discussed, is that unmanaged pressure corrupts the behaviors of even the smartest and most well-meaning bosses, generating reactivity and resentment that consume both them and the people who work for them.

The key word there is *unmanaged*.

Pressure is inescapable when you're the one in charge. Whether you run a global corporation or a local food bank, you have to contend with the pressures of driving your organization's agenda while at the same time navigating time and resource limitations, meeting expectations, fielding demands, finding and retaining the right talent, holding up morale without compromising results, and handling snafus, not to mention keeping an eye toward future strategy and growth. Even if you're not running the organization, pressure starts to build with more responsibility.

The higher up you go, the more intense that becomes. To meet this rise in pressure head-on and guide your team with a steady hand, you need to regulate your reactions to that intensity. Someone, somewhere, somehow will always fall short of your expectations. Resources you thought you had at your disposal will vanish like free snacks at 4 p.m. Employees will make mistakes; colleagues will do whatever it is they do that pisses you off. At times, the demands on you will exceed what you can humanly accomplish without cloning yourself. Those are givens outside your control.

The emotions that get stirred up in the face of those pressures are also not always easy to control. We're human, we have emotional reactions to events. The variable that is within your control, however, is how you respond. Okay, so you're irritated, scared that you won't meet the mark, or overwhelmed. Got it. That can happen. Even as those emotions swirl up, do you keep a cool head or—knowingly or unknowingly—turn into the boss from hell?

This is where self-regulation comes into play.

Your ability to self-regulate your inner response to external pressure makes all the difference at work and in life. You still may feel whatever you are feeling—you're just able to recognize why, which shifts you out of the amygdala takeover of fight-or-flight and back into more reasoned, productive thinking. Rather than taking swipes that undermine an underperforming employee's future performance and morale, you can address them firmly yet with respect, coaching them to more productive results. You can assuage the client, pivot from the lost deal to the next opportunity, think through alternatives to compensate for a resource gap. You've got this.

Part Four illuminates the internal forces that make it difficult to meet those external forces with composure and a clear head. These forces form what I call Pressure Pitfalls, aka hazards that become dangerous when unheeded and leave us vulnerable in high-pressure moments. That's when we get provoked into a full-blown amygdala hijack as our inner Mr. Hyde wreaks havoc on our behaviors.

These Mr. Hyde behaviors fall into one of three categories:

1. **Controlling** the situation or others (*I have no time for others' mistakes, I'll just do it myself*)
2. **Abdicating**, aka the blame game (*It's YOUR fault . . . you screwed this up . . .*)
3. **Automating** to your familiar Singular Story (*Sorry not sorry, this is how I do things*)

When in the grips of heightened emotions, even someone with first-class people skills reverts to one of these three behaviors. This is precisely how Benita ended up commanding an employee during a crisis-generated deadline to "put on his big boy pants" and stay through the weekend to get a report done. Ouch.

Unmanaged pressure is contagious, cycling around in infectious loops like an airborne virus. If you think about the fact that you, as the boss, are the primary source of pressure for your team, you'll see just how directly your ability to deal with pressure impacts everyone else. Your pressure outbursts trigger those same fight-or-flight responses in them, impairing their productivity and possibly their well-being, which simply boomerangs back to you and your pressure pile. So I'll tell the most growly Mr. Hydes that yes, sure, you may make a huge impact for the company, but how much *more* could you generate if you self-regulated instead of spewing unchecked pressure on your team? Again and again, when I work with executives who are frustrated by the seeming disconnection between their effort and the team's motivation, the culprit is their own behavior.

The pressure crush corrupts our best traits, reaching even our most prized skills. Let's say, for instance, that you have a known talent for pitching ideas to potential clients. When pressure impacts your ability to think clearly, that talent can easily devolve into a toxic cocktail of sticking to your conclusions as the only truth, hogging the microphone, not pausing to see what others already know, constantly referencing your past, and doling out obvious truths as valuable advice. A bitter tonic for your team to swallow.

Unmanaged pressure leaks out in ways we don't anticipate. I see so many people whose marriages are in disarray because they come home and take out their frustrations on their family, yelling at a child for not eating their broccoli when what they are angry about has nothing to do with veggies. Some turn the force onto themselves—cardiologists and addiction specialists are familiar with this coping mechanism. Others begin taking liberties beyond what they are entitled to when their self-regulating abilities aren't there to keep their baser instincts in check.

To be clear: when I say "pressure," I don't mean "stress." Stress is how you feel, often in response to pressure, internalized as a bodily experience. Some experts say stress is good because it sharpens focus, but when you remain in a stressed state for long periods of time, you bathe your organs in cortisol, the stress hormone scientifically proven to impair clear thinking and cause health issues. Pressure, however, is an external force coming at you and then recycled into what you're generating and spewing outward. I'm not here to tell you to take more vacations or dilute your power. You do, however, need to learn to modulate your response to pressure productively.

I imagine the *"yeah, but"* alarm bells are already clamoring in your head. *Yeah, but I've heard this all before. Yeah, but who has time for this? Yeah, but real winners are tough, they can withstand the pressure. Yeah, but I've learned to power through, and I'm doing just fine.* These beliefs are exactly what land so many executives in trouble and in need of my services.

The following chapters highlight the most common Pressure Pitfalls I've witnessed my clients fall prey to. By assessing when and where these traps appear in your current behaviors, you can apply the specific detailed tools to steer clear of them.

CHAPTER NINE

Spot Your Hidden Triggers

The year 2007 was jam-packed for me. I was a year and a half into building my new business as an independent executive coach and had a preschooler and a toddler at home. I was also the sole earner for my family at the time, which extended to taking care of my mother, who was in an assisted-living facility with steadily advancing Alzheimer's. The pressures on me were intense.

One ordinary gray October day in Seattle, as I was getting ready to meet a client, I was hit by a wave of dizziness and chalked it up to not having eaten yet. So I ate breakfast, sat still for a bit, declared myself fine, and went to my meeting. But my body wasn't done. On my return drive, the nausea returned so forcefully I had to pull over and throw up. I somehow made it back home and spent the rest of the day in bed with a violently spinning head.

This was the first case of what became chronic and crippling episodes of vertigo. For the first few years, when the attacks occurred, they were so extreme I couldn't move, talk, or even open my eyes without throwing up because the room spun so forcefully. Being someone at that time who refused to slow down, this was my body's way of shutting me down completely.

These attacks became a predictable response to stress for me. The vertigo would follow high-stress events. When our beloved dog, Brio, died and his lifeless body was being taken out of our home, my son Zaref asked if I was going to get vertigo. Sure enough, two days later, I was hit with an attack.

I still get these attacks from time to time, but nowhere near as extreme or with the same level of regularity. I've learned to notice the very early signs: something on a cellular level just feels "off," and like a tiny glitch in the Matrix, I feel a slight lurch in my step, a passing shadow of blurriness, a touch of clamminess on my forehead. The second these warnings appear, I immediately cancel my day, take my meds, and set myself up in bed with the supplies I need of carbonated water and dry toast. I don't resist the signs, and the episodes pass much easier.

Much in the same way, we can steer clear of Pressure Pitfalls by recognizing our trigger warnings *before* we get activated by them. The Trigger Spotter tool helps you identify your personal signals so you can unhook from the charge of emotions in the moment they occur and change course.

Trigger Spotter: Identify What Activates You

To manage pressure in real time, this tool enables you to drill down into what specifically (and usually unintentionally) sets you off course into "bad boss" behaviors. Use this tool when:

- You have received feedback that you are too hard on your employees (the number one issue that shows up in 360s)
- You are frequently angered, irritated, disappointed, fearful, anxious
- Your responses to difficult situations feel beyond your control
- Your negative response to a situation is much stronger than the situation merits

Put It into Practice

Step One: Identify your Pressure Points

Like vertigo, amygdala attacks usually come with situational prompts and telltale warning signs. The following coaching questions can help you identify your pressure triggers so you can be aware of when they are most likely to show up:

- **What general scenarios do I find most stressful?** These might include spotlight situations such as giving presentations or running meetings, social dynamics like navigating interpersonal conflicts, receiving or giving critical feedback, tight deadlines, or dealing with unexpected urgencies. If you aren't sure, think back to the last few times you behaved in a way that you're not proud of and track it to what was going on at that moment.

- **What types of people tend to put me on high alert?** Your boss? Clients? Employees who underperform? A manipulative colleague? People who indulge in verbal overkill?

- **What tends to get under my skin the most?** Is it when you get interrupted? Are lied or talked down to? When someone is late or cancels at the last minute? How about when someone claims credit for your work or neglects to include you in the information flow? Alternatively, maybe non-interpersonal annoyances like technology glitches, travel hiccups, and bureaucratic red tape get your blood boiling.

- **What days of the week or cyclical or seasonal times are particularly pressure-filled for me?** This could be anything from a weekly meeting or deadline to an annual conference, year-end review, or pre-event preparation.

- **When are the moments I am not at my best?** When you're sleep-deprived? Hungry? In the mornings before you've had your coffee or late afternoons when your energy dips?

- **What do I experience physically when I get triggered?** Trigger warnings of anger, fear, or other powerful emotions usually come with a physical cue, like a rapid heartbeat, stomach churning, flushed face or heat in the tips of your ears, clenched teeth or fists, or a throbbing sensation in your temples.

Step Two: Design your Hijack Neutralizers

Just as experts advise we create an action plan for our families in case of a natural disaster, you want to create a plan for what you'll do in the moment when your personal pressure points activate an amygdala hijack. Having a go-to set of Hijack Neutralizers enables you to shift out of prehistoric fight-or-flight brain and back into a powerful mindset.

Scientifically proven methods to deactivate the amygdala include:

- Actively engage the rational part of your brain for six seconds by doing slightly complex math (say, counting backward from one hundred by seven). This moves your thoughts out of the threatened primitive brain and back to the prefrontal cortex, where you can access clear thinking and reasoning.

- Engage in a working-memory task, which again directs the brain back to executive functioning. According to the National Institutes of Health, working memory is "the retention of a small amount of information in readily-accessible form." Examples of working memory tasks are recalling your childhood address, thinking through the daily itinerary of a past trip, or recalling the lyrics of your favorite song.

- Take five slow, deep breaths all the way down to your belly. Brain science shows we can, within moments, alter our mental state through physiological regulation. Just as an amygdala hijack causes a physiological reaction in which our breath becomes more shallow and rapid, we can reverse engineer our way back to calm through changing our breathing pattern.

- Use the 5-4-3-2-1 grounding exercise developed by Dr. Helen Hendriksen, clinical psychologist at Boston University. Identify five things you can see, four things you can hear, three things you can touch, two things you can smell, and one thing you can taste. By focusing on the present through the surround-scape of your senses, you divert your mind from roiling thoughts.

- Describe (in your head or in writing) what's happening without any interpretation or judgment. For instance, "I am feeling the urge to throw something in response to Ellen's comment." In cognitive behavior therapy this is known as thought challenging, in which you shift out of your insider perspective of "the truth"—in this case your "truth" might be "Ellen said something stupid!"—and into a more objective one.

Or you may choose a personalized mechanism that you know works for you. Some of my clients drink a full glass of water to cool off or take a lap around the office to burn off energy. Others, like Viola, whom you will read about below, use a mnemonic (a sentence where the first letter of each word stands for an action you will take) that spells out their Hijack Neutralizers for specific situations. Whatever you choose, the essential part is to have it ready to pull out when your triggers get tripped.

Case Study: Trigger Spotting in Action

Viola was tough on herself and even tougher on her staff. One of the most damning critiques in Viola's 360 was that anytime she was offered a suggestion or asked a question she deemed "worthless," she would respond with a harshness that damaged her employees' trust in her, not to mention their morale.

Once Viola realized that the formidable pressure she was under was activating this hurtful impatience—not to mention the blood pressure spikes her doctor repeatedly warned her about—she established an in-the-moment solution. Viola's first step was to recognize her situational irritants and physical cues. We established four scenarios that were consistent hot spots for her: the weekly staff meeting, sloppy written work from her team, when someone did not disclose a trouble area until it was too far down the road, and people who tried to make up an answer on the spot when they didn't have one instead of saying they'd get back to her. Her physical cues that she was getting triggered included removing her glasses to rub her eyes and clamping her lips closed (sometimes even drawing blood as she bit down on the inside of her lip to try to contain an emotional outburst).

From there, Viola used a mnemonic a friend gave her to activate her Hijack Neutralizers and inform the steps she would follow: in the moment Viola would recall, "lazy creeks run past dazzling waterfalls," or LCRPDWF, and employ the most relevant technique from the list.

- **Listen** through to the full stop; do not interrupt
- **Confirm** by paraphrasing what you heard
- **Refer** the question or suggestion to someone else; allow others to address it if they're able
- **Prepare** your response; don't give a knee-jerk answer right away

- **Don't** respond in depth; just say, "That's an interesting point (or question)"
- **Waffle**; say, "I need to think about this longer; my first response is in this direction, but I reserve the right to change my mind"
- **Flee** before failure (I often say to my clients: it's better for you to cancel the meeting rather than show up in a crappy mood an hour after your red-eye flight lands)

After a few months of deploying these Hijack Neutralizers, Viola's outbursts decreased dramatically. Inversely, the relationship with her team improved, along with her blood pressure.

 Trigger Spotting Micro Habit

At the end of the workday, take thirty seconds to review your day and record moments your emotions ran high, noting what caused them. Which events hooked you? What thoughts came up? What did you say or do, and what resulted? After a few weeks, you can look back and will undoubtedly start to see repeating patterns.

CHAPTER TEN

Root Out Unmet Hungers

When someone disappoints you, do you speak up? When you want to say no, do you find yourself saying yes? When someone cuts you off in traffic, do you lose it sometimes? Do you feel wounded when a coworker is critical of your choices? Do you become irritated, despondent, or avoid dealing with people who work for you when they don't perform in the ways you expect?

We are human, and every one of us is driven by unmet hungers. I'm not speaking of physical hungers, but strong emotional and psychological needs. These inner needs pull on us ever so slightly (or not so slightly) and unconsciously drive our actions. Wanting to be liked or to belong, longing to be seen and heard, seeking praise—these are deep-seated hungers, often formed long ago. As therapist Vienna Pharaon writes in *The Origins of You: How Breaking Family Patterns Can Liberate the Way We Live and Love*, we all encounter some sense of wounding in our families of origin. These wounds lead us to compensate in specific ways: by performing, pleasing, hiding, hoarding, avoiding, and so on. They create our human desires to please, to matter, to be appreciated, to belong, to be important, to be right, to be the smartest or the funniest. Someone, somewhere, at some time behaved in ways that led us to conclude that love equaled one of these measures, and this shaped us and our view of the world. We spend the rest of our lives feeding that hunger over and over.

When we're younger, feeding our hungers equates to emotional survival. As adults, we're more robust and may be better at modulating our responses, but those small hungers still drive the bus. No matter how evolved we are, how many hours of therapy we've logged, books on emotional intelligence we've read, or spiritual retreats we've attended, when we're pushed out of our comfort zone, these hungers take over, bringing out the wee ravenous beasties in us. When we're corrupted by pressure, those hungers take over and trigger reactivity.

Take Mina, for instance, who began struggling in her new C-level role almost right away. We quickly ascertained that when Mina takes on any new project, she goes very deep into the details for a long time—too long. As the chief technology officer of a $100 million company, that doesn't fly. She received feedback that she needed to become more strategic and fast. Using the Hunger Tracker, which you'll find at the end of this section, we discovered the unseen hunger where she was getting stuck. As the daughter of Chinese immigrants who demanded perfection from their children, Mina was driven by a need to prove herself over and over. To step back and trust her team to handle the details felt like a threat not only to her precise standards but to her entire identity. Despite having one of the most reputable engineering teams in the business, she would stay up until the early morning hours poring over every line of code just to get the hit of knowing she was delivering unassailably flawless material. Mina's perfectionism was exacerbated by a second all-too-common hunger (there's usually more than just one): to be liked. She wouldn't even give her team the minutiae to deal with, because what would happen if they didn't do it right? Then she'd have to give them tough feedback, the thought of which turned her stomach. Mina piled the work onto herself and burrowed into it to feed both those underlying hungers.

On the other hand, my client Jonas is driven by a different hunger.

An economist known on the international stage, he is invited regularly to be on councils with world leaders and testify before Congress. Many people mention Jonas's self importance, but I think there's an unmet need beneath that attitude. Having learned about the formative years that shaped how he approached the world, I see Jonas's behavior as reflecting a need never to miss an opportunity to seen, by being everywhere at once. Others interpret his fear of missing out as arrogant self-promotion.

Driven by fear, Jonas is reluctant to turn down any invitation or let go of any responsibilities. Even though he advises heads of state, he holds on to minor tasks that he has no business doing. For example, he helped start a steering committee for an initiative that is now thriving. Two years ago, I asked him, "Do you still need to be part of this? Can it run without you?"

"You're right, you're right," he told me.

"You don't need to leave entirely," I clarified. "But do you need to still be the person who convenes every meeting and solves every issue?"

"No," he replied. "I don't. But . . ."

He's still running that committee today.

Jonas is stuck in a sticky trap that a former Microsoft manager named Brad Abrams called "peanut buttering." Abrams defined peanut buttering as a tendency to spread resources thinly across a large number of projects instead of concentrating them on a few key ones. In Jonas's case, he spreads himself across commitments, even time zones. Not surprisingly, this waters down his ability to give 100 percent to any one effort or even a few concentrated projects that would move the needle the most.

Being present requires a level of self-awareness about the hungers that drive you. These hungers can be uncomfortable to unpack. For Jonas, the discomfort lay in being labeled "weird" as a kid and shunted to the shadows of obscurity. Despite having a Ph.D. and influencing international policies as an adult, that marginalized eight-year-old still crept into his psyche. He has an almost bottomless hunger to say yes and keep all the toys for himself. As I told Jonas, if we don't peek inside that inner toy chest and understand what is driving us so we can comfort it and then disconnect from it, we are doomed to repeat the spiral of good intentions but failed ambitions. Root out the hungers and their saboteurs lose their hold over you and your reactions. When you understand your hungers, you'll be able to recognize when you're getting triggered—*and then stop the behavior in its tracks*. This is mindfulness at its best, stepping outside your reactive emotionality in highly pressurized moments and rationally seeing all the puzzle pieces.

How do you know you're in hunger territory? If your reaction is bigger or more intense than the situation warrants, it's a clue that something deeper is going on.

My client Jun, for instance, came to our coaching session looking visibly shaken, raking her hands through her short black hair and leading with "This is bad, Sabina. Bad."

"What's wrong?" I asked, concerned. Jun is highly respected in her field and someone I'd always known to be even-keeled, even a bit aloof.

"They want to promote me," she replied.

"Okayyyy," I said. "And . . . ?"

"I'm terrified. All these old white guys are going to promote me just so they can take me down."

Jun had had no experience of racial or gender discrimination at work before, nor had she witnessed any in her time at the company. Granted, there are always cultural biases at play, but this speculation was one she had whipped up in her own terrified imagination. As we talked, we uncovered a fear the exact opposite of Jonas's: Jun was deathly afraid of standing in the limelight. The story came out that she grew up in the Midwest as the only person of Japanese origin in her class. Her classmates would spit at her, scratch her, call her racially charged names, so she learned to play small as a means of self-protection. I congratulated Jun for calling out this hunger at the beginning of her next-level journey. Without this knowledge in hand, when the pressure skyrocketed to ten, she would have automated to her default behavior. Forget about those old guys—Jun would have done a great job diminishing her power all on her own.

In case you need more motivation to figure out which hungers drive you: I promise people who work for you already know them and are tapping them to their best advantage. A colleague of mine—I'll call her Alyson—shared a story of a boss she had early in her career whose monstrous ego entered the room ten feet ahead of his obnoxiously loud voice. He would walk around pointing out his expensive new Italian loafers and showing pictures of the grandiose home he was building on a Caribbean island. Alyson understood that his voracious need for praise and admiration stemmed from deep personal insecurity.

"I hate to admit this," she told me, "but we all kind of preyed on that. We knew if we needed something from him, we'd need to start with praise to grease the wheels, and he'd be all ears. It was kind of sad, actually—I felt badly for him—but he was so horrible and abusive to his entire staff that I didn't feel *that* bad."

You're probably thinking, *Oh, I would know if I had a blind spot that big.* But would you? They're called blind spots for a reason.

Harvard psychologists Robert Kegan and Lisa Laskow Lahey developed the Immunity to Change framework to illuminate the powerful, hidden forces (aka hungers) that keep us from making changes. Through their work I learned that these hidden hungers are a powerful deterrent to change. As soon as pressure rises, our hungers take over. No matter what we say about our intentions, we will remain immune to change until we recognize and address these hungers. Identifying our unmet hungers is the first step toward change.

Inspired by their work, I created a Hunger Tracker diagnostic to help clients identify the most common hungers that unconsciously drive them. This diagnostic outlined below will enable you also to reverse engineer your behaviors and diagnose the unmet hungers that may be driving you. Once you see your hungers in action, you're better able to feed them in healthier ways and move past your immunity to change.

The Hunger Tracker: Identify the Hidden Needs Driving You

Behaviors	Narratives: I tell myself . . .	Hunger
I speak more often and longer than others in meetings I interrupt others I get impatient, shake my head, or cut someone off while they are describing a new idea	*I know the answers* *They don't get it* *I can make meetings go faster by cutting to the chase because I have a long track record of success and have seen it all before*	To be seen as the smartest/most insightful/most experienced person in the room
I tell heroic tales about myself (how I saved the day, landed the client, fixed the problem, etc.) I name-drop I exaggerate and garnish I feel compelled to one-up other people's narratives and center attention back on myself	*I deserve to be noticed* *If prominent people praise me, I matter* *I have to stay out front to make sure I'm noticed*	To feel relevant
I don't delegate I'm always on I jump in to help without asking if others need help I go out of my way to help others even at cost to me and my family I check my devices nonstop even during family time	*I'm the only one who can do this right* *It'll take me less time to just do this myself* *Everyone else is busy, I don't want to burden them* *If I am needed, I am indispensable* *If I am indispensable, I am safe in my job*	To be needed
I'm the first to respond in every meeting, email thread, and online post I dictate a timeline to my team without checking if it's reasonable for them I don't ask others for their opinion I state things are going well even when I suspect they aren't If I delegate, I check in frequently or redo the work once others have submitted it to me	*If I don't respond right away, people will solve things in ways that are not great* *If I'm not steering the ship, I'll be left off it* *If I ask how others are feeling/thinking, it'll open a can of worms and distract from getting things done* *I know best*	To be in control

Behaviors	Narratives: I tell myself . . .	Hunger
I take offense easily I view others' actions as personal attacks I'm quick to assign blame to others rather than myself I don't ever offer to clean up after an event, take notes, or schedule meetings on behalf of the team I secretly resent it when one of my colleagues is praised for their accomplishments; I'm slower to add my congratulations and am rarely curious about their work or how they did it I make sure people know I have a Ph.D. I run chronically late to every meeting	*How dare they question me?* *They have no idea how much I know/have done* *If I engage in trivial tasks, people will not respect my thought leadership; they will ask me to volunteer for other trivial tasks and my calendar will be mired in minutiae* *I deserve the recognition more than my colleagues* *My time is more important than theirs*	To be seen as important
I am the first to respond to emails and messages I say yes to everything even if it's not a priority for me I volunteer for every committee or task I agree to all after-work events even at the cost of family time or my own self-care I work throughout my vacations	*If I'm not at a meeting, people might think or talk about me negatively* *If I say no to smaller items, people won't ask me to work on more exciting projects because they'll assume I'm too busy* *I need to just buckle down because this is temporary, it will be easier next quarter*	To never miss out on anything
I don't verbalize disagreement I say yes even when I'd rather say no I pepper my emails with niceties, flattery, and emojis I ask for others' opinions repeatedly when the decision is mine to make If someone pushes back, instead of laying out the facts, I say, "Let me look into that" My to-do list is overflowing with communications I put off to avoid confronting an uncomfortable issue	*If others are unhappy with me, they won't invite me to their meetings or give me interesting projects* *I will appear rude and ungrateful if I disagree* *If I am assertive in my opinions, others will think I am pushy* *If they don't like me, I'll be cast aside*	To be liked by everyone at all times

Behaviors	Narratives: I tell myself . . .	Hunger
I don't speak up in meetings I do nearly all the work behind the scenes but then am overly generous in crediting others for their effort I take on more than my fair share of administrative tasks for the group: ordering lunch, taking notes, and doing other trivial errands I do the work behind the scenes but then ask my colleagues to present at executive or team meetings	*If I don't stick out, I can't be criticized* *If I speak up, people will realize how much I don't know or that I don't measure up* *If I take credit for work I've done, then I will receive all the blame when things don't go well* *I never want anyone to find fault with anything I do*	To play small and stay safe
I don't say yes to anything unless I know I can deliver it flawlessly I take longer to complete tasks than promised because I'm constantly redoing, double-checking, and polishing my work I shut down and don't speak up when criticized	*If I perform flawlessly, I am beyond reproach* *If I make a mistake, it means I'm no good and therefore disposable* *If someone else finds fault in my work, they'll think I'm incompetent*	To be perfect
I'm quick to assign blame for any issues to others I never apologize I go on lengthy rants about "those idiots in the other department" I don't start things because I'm often waiting for someone else to say or do something *(if only they would complete their part and hand it to me . . .)* I don't take personal time for self-care but complain about being overworked/tired/ burned out	*If I take accountability, then I will be responsible for fixing problems and will buckle under the weight of it all* *If I'm at fault, no one will like me or want me on their team* *If I'm at fault, I'll look stupid, incompetent* *If I did take time to do something for myself, I'd be seen as selfish and not revered as a martyr*	To be a victim

Case Study: The Hunger Tracker in Action

What do you do once you recognize your unmet hungers?

Once Mina (whom you met on page 160) realized her drive to be perfect (and perfectly liked and approved of by everyone) was taking charge in high-pressure situations, she followed these three steps:

- **Observe.** Mina simply watched her hungers in action for two weeks to move her reactions from unconscious to conscious. She noticed that whenever someone didn't smile and nod while she was speaking, she would assume they didn't like her idea. As a result, she would backpedal and come across as someone who lacked conviction. Mina also noticed that the more senior someone was in the hierarchy, the less likely she was to disagree with them even if she felt certain of her stance.

- **Examine.** From there, Mina dug into the narratives behind these hungers (the second column in the Hunger Tracker) to assess if they were fact or self-generated fiction. For example, Mina isolated the thought *If I make a mistake, it means I'm no good and therefore disposable.* The corresponding action usually entailed her spending long hours perfecting her work and living in fear that it would not measure up. She was able to identify two instances that week in which her manager had given her feedback on how to improve a presentation. Far from firing her, her manager had mentioned how insightful Mina had been in her analysis. Mina was able to see objectively how her all-or-nothing narrative was flawed, generating unnecessary anxiety and costing her valuable time as she triple- and quadruple-checked her work to ensure it was perfect.

- **Experiment.** Lastly, Mina created a small experiment to see what would happen if she interrupted her default reaction. While working on a low-stakes project, she set a timer for when she would submit her work. This prevented her from wasting excessive time perfecting low-priority work and gave her the chance to see that her product was just as good without the excessive checking and rechecking. On the rare occasions when she would make a mistake, Mina was relieved to discover nothing terrible happened if she was a fraction less than perfect. As you may recall when we talked about Micro Habits, we build resilience through recovering from failure; that is how we build better adaptive responses to pressure. In Mina's case, she was able to de-escalate her tendency to catastrophize under pressure and drastically reduce her hunger-driven anxieties.

CHAPTER ELEVEN

Steer Clear of the Sole Provider Trap

"You're one of the two best test managers in all of Microsoft."

You might think hearing these words from my boss would have made me do a victory dance. Instead, I realized I'd made the biggest mistake of my career.

The year was 1997, and I was the manager of a large team responsible for testing key products including Windows and Internet Explorer. After years of running test teams, I was eager to take on new challenges. While I loved the detective part of testing, seeking out and fixing hidden bugs to improve products for a better customer experience, I was yearning to become a program manager and design those products from the ground up. I went to my boss, Tom, to discuss opportunities along those lines. Tom's remark about my being one of the top two test managers in the company was both a compliment (*yay me!*) and a reason why he needed me to remain in that role (*uh-oh*). That's when I realized I'd worked so hard to become indispensable that I'd sabotaged my own career growth.

I fell into the same Sole Provider trap my clients regularly visit today.

The second Pressure Pitfall of believing we need to do it all sneaks up on us. Being a Sole Provider starts with a commonsense work ethic of excellence. When starting out, we set an expectation for ourselves to have all the answers and know more about our domain than others. We're hypervigilant about being on top of all the details. We mobilize all our inner resources to deliver quickly and flawlessly. There's no question that self-motivation and self-reliance are vital tools for getting ahead. Then, when we step up into a role of authority, we continue with those practices, but as you now know from the first chapter, what once were our best practices are not the same ones we need when we move to the next level. Obscured by Power Gaps and triggered by untended Pressure Pitfalls, self-reliance takes an abrupt turn into self-absorption, competitiveness, and righteousness.

At their best, Sole Providers are infused with take-charge energy. They believe (often rightly so) that they are the ones with all the answers—the ones who know how to produce to a high level of excellence with maximum efficiency. With deep institutional knowledge, keen analytic skills, attention to detail, and dedication to follow-through, Sole Providers take the lead on everything from innovating to executing. "I've got this" is the cornerstone of their work ethic.

Behind the wizard's curtain, however, is often a bubbling cauldron of frustration, resentment, and stress. What Sole Providers really mean when they say "I've got this" is "I'm the *only one* who's got this, so I need to do it." They tell themselves stories like *I'm the lead on this, so I'm responsible . . . I'm the only one who knows how to do this right . . . It's my job to take care of my team; I'll just do it so they aren't overburdened.* Delegating? They know of course it's smart practice, but they either don't do it or, when they do, end up aggravated because their team doesn't generate the results they'd hoped for. Doing everything themselves is their defining trait. Unsurprisingly, they're often overwhelmed and overworked, perpetually at risk of tipping into "bad boss" behaviors.

As authors Ronald Heifetz and Marty Linsky explain, people look to their bosses to protect them from the changing agendas in the corporate world and the vagaries of schedules, to provide order to roles, priorities, responsibilities, and resources, and clear directives so they know what's expected of them and how they can measure success. Undoubtedly, the more power you gain in any organization, the greater the expectations on you to provide protection, order, and direction for the people on your team. The Sole Provider, however, takes this one step further, from protection to stifling, from order to control, from providing direction to becoming the air traffic controller, pilot, and engine mechanic all wrapped into one. They suck up uncompleted tasks to save their people from being overworked and absorb harsh criticism or unreasonable demands from other teams or senior management to shield their team from corporate storms. They do all this under various umbrellas, from "It's my job" to "I'm trying to be a good shield for my people" to "I'm the only one who can get this done right/fast/well, so I'll just do it myself." But there's much more at play here under the surface than we may realize.

The need to do it all is driven by a survival instinct. Fueled by fear of being rendered irrelevant, we fiercely protect our corporate shelf life. Consciously or not, we want to be seen as heroes who are indispensable, and we live out that desire by building ultimate dependence on ourselves.

How do we build this dependence, exactly? Rather than coach our team to develop skills and competence of their own—what I call "vitamins"—we dole out quick fixes and solutions as painkillers. We refuse to let them learn through experimentation and failure and build their own muscles. Easy answers keep our undernourished team coming back for more and more, proving how needed we are. Sole Providers often end their workdays depleted and demoralized but assured they'll live to see another day of corporate relevance. The primal survival need runs deep.

Heroic actions are further cemented into the system because it thrives on us buying into our own mythology. As a direct report to one of my clients told me, "I'll admit we love when Mandana provides all the solutions and ideas. It means we can do less and not risk being wrong." If we do the heavy lifting often enough, our teams come to rely on that—then we wonder why no one else can do the work the way we need it done.

Sucking up all the work alienates and stunts the growth of those who work for a Sole Provider, widening the Power Gap. More than any other behavior, Sole Provider tendencies will eat away at your calendar, capacities, and opportunities for advancement. They drain your time, patience, energy, and—if left unchecked—the sense of purpose and joy that drove your success until now. We all have natural boundaries within us that allow us to withstand pressure; if we didn't, we'd crumple under the first deadline or critique that came our way. Next-level pressures, however, demand stronger boundaries.

The Sole Provider plays a variety of overfunctioning roles. I've outlined below the four most common types: the Caretaker, the Whack-a-Mole Champ, the Flash, and the Straight-A Student. Like many of my clients, you may recognize yourself in one or more of these—they aren't mutually exclusive.

The Caretaker

As a PR manager at an insurance company, Ariana dedicated a lot of energy to seeking out the inner competence of everyone who worked for and with her. Her 360 revealed a knack for asking powerful questions to evoke innovation, such as "If there were no barriers, how would you address this problem right now?" It also revealed that she gave clear directives on any mission and her expectations, often detailed in an email that ended with "Please reach out to me directly if you would like any further clarity." After that, she would step back and trust her team to execute, providing guidance when necessary. Ariana embodied many of the top strengths I hear cited in 360 reviews: intelligent, effective in communication, able to deliver results, strategic, and excellent at managing interpersonal dynamics.

This is what healthy caretaking as a boss looks like. The myriad skills it encompasses, from fostering innovation to supporting the

mental well-being of one's team, have been proven crucial for successful leadership. Like all human traits, however, the caretaking urge has
a positive and negative expression. When a manager is rooted in the
healthy end of the caretaking continuum, they serve as both a guide
and a coach. It takes an unhealthy turn when the caretaking becomes
disabling, both for the people who work for them and the Caretaker
themselves.

Take Daniel, for instance, who landed squarely on the disabling
end of the spectrum. As the oldest of seven siblings, caretaking came
naturally to this kind soul. Daniel was the person everyone at the office turned to for advice or to commiserate with about situations gone
awry. He once relayed to me with a sweet smile that someone had re-
ferred to him as "the resident teddy bear." At six-foot-five with a 250-
pound frame and warm brown eyes, the nickname seemed fitting.

The problem was that Daniel wasn't a stuffed comfort toy—he was
an accounting manager of a manufacturing company. The success of
his operation depended on careful attention to every decimal point and
weekly reports for the CFO. That meant he needed his colleagues from
other departments to submit their invoices on time, filled out correctly
and thoroughly, and his team to input the information similarly. But
none of this was happening. Instead, with regularity at least one of his
four accountants would call with a personal situation that prevented
them from getting their reports in on time, knowing Daniel would
understand. Other times they would spend upward of an hour in his
office venting about whatever was going wrong with their current project. Daniel would nod sympathetically, not letting on that behind his
kind smile and compassionate murmurs was a sinking feeling of dread,
knowing he would have to step in and do the work for them. Week after
week, Daniel would send "gentle reminder" emails to his colleagues to
submit their expenses, most of which would come in late or be so sloppy
that Daniel would need to chase down the details to correct them.

When I asked him why he didn't express his dismay about this or
have one of his direct reports do the detailed work of fixing the ex-

penses, Daniel replied, "Oh, I know they're super busy. I don't want to put any more stress on them."

Kind? Certainly. But productive? Not in the least.

Caretakers like Daniel, who tip into enabling, sabotage valuable reserves of time and bandwidth and the agency of those who work with them. When protection morphs into control, the Caretaker becomes what psychologist Stephen Karpman refers to as the "rescuer" in the Drama Triangle model he developed. The Drama Triangle explains three common, unhealthy ways people respond to conflict: the victim (in this case, the worker who is stressed), the persecutor (could be the client, the big boss, an external event . . . whoever or whatever is generating the pressure), and the rescuer (you guessed it, the Caretaker). The rescuer appears to ease the suffering of the victim. On the surface, it looks like they are being sympathetic, but really, they are just keeping the victim trapped in the "poor me" cycle by adopting a "poor you" attitude. The Caretaker treats team members as though they need rescuing. Ironically, the more time a Caretaker spends rescuing others, the easier it is for them to tip into victimhood and feel taken advantage of.

In our first session together, my client Julia remarked with a heavy sigh, "My office might as well have a revolving door, so many people come in and out needing answers." As Julia and I continued to work together, I came to understand her as a deeply caring person much like Daniel. It became evident that she had not only installed that figurative revolving door, but regularly greased the hinges. The reason her team kept popping in was because she was doling out painkillers rather than vitamins. Julia would fix any problem that arose. It made me think of a parent bandaging up a skinned knee and sending their child back out to ride the very same bike they didn't really know how to operate, only to have the child return again sobbing because they had been merely patched up, not taught how to balance and pedal on their own.

Caretakers rely on noble stories to justify their actions. They willingly step into a sacrifice sinkhole telling themselves things like *I have to do this for the sake of my team/clients/company . . . It's my job to make sure my team is happy . . . They're too overworked as it is. I can't burden them more, so I'll just skip my workout/kid's soccer game/vacation and get this done.*

All these may be true, but behind many noble stories lurks that primal need for self-protection around our own relevance, along with a personalized menu of other unmet hungers. A lot of times we make decisions on behalf of other people and tell ourselves virtuous stories about why, when in truth we're doing it to skirt around discomfort. "I figured you were busy, so I'd take it off your plate" when really what's under there is "I didn't want to tell you that you suck at it, so I'll just do it myself." Sure, we get to avoid interpersonal friction, but at what cost?

A rescuing manager is often driven by a hunger to be liked (dare I even say loved?) by everyone. We want our team to be happy, to go home and declare us the best boss they've ever had. Our desire to meet their need for protection, order, and direction is sincere, so we go way above and beyond, often to our detriment and theirs.

The Caretaker is a benevolent soul with the best of intentions, no question about that. But we can be a good boss and be caring *without* veering into ineffective management or doing damage to our well-being.

Coaching Consideration: Are You a Caretaker?

A useful diagnostic to determine if you're in Caretaker territory is to listen to the story you're telling yourself about why you're jumping in. If the story hinges on justifying your role (*It's my job*), saving them (*I don't want them to fail* or *I don't want to burden them*), or efficiency (*I'll just do it myself to get it done*), you know you're in emotionally fraught territory. The more noble the story, the more hooked you are.

The Whack-a-Mole Champ

Cezar was prized for his calmness under pressure and outstanding ability to solve thorny issues. Newly promoted to manager in a services firm, Cezar eagerly tackled every issue that came his way—and there were plenty. The company's archaic pen-and-paper tracking systems were riddled with errors, and each day brought a new challenge that had to be resolved yesterday. With every fresh crisis, Cezar donned his superhero cape, swooped in to rally his team without explaining the bigger picture of what was happening or what was needed ("Too complicated to explain, just go!"), and saved the day. He went to bed each night sleeping secure in the knowledge they had solved the problem, only to repeat the cycle the next day.

I liken this to the carnival game of Whack-a-Mole. If you've never played it, it's a fast-paced game that demands high energy and lightning-fast reflexes. Beneath a large board filled with holes are little plastic moles that pop up quickly and at random, again and again. Each player is given a rubber mallet, and when the bell rings, they must frantically whack the moles down as fast as they pop up. The person who thumps the highest number of moles within sixty seconds is the winner.

Like all Whack-a-Mole champs, Cezar was addicted to the dopamine rush of the game. With every fire he put out at work, he got another hit of the feel-good chemical coursing through his brain. Rather than stepping back and trying to rework the underlying issues, he stayed in the fray to get the hit not just from the dopamine, but the praise; after all, we reward firefighters, not fire preventers.

Like the Caretaker, there are positive and negative expressions of the Whack-a-Mole Champ. On the positive side, these champs are ace problem solvers who can fashion a solution out of the proverbial paper clip and stick of chewing gum. Quick on their feet and in command, they're the ones you want in an emergency. Whack-a-Mole Champs are always in motion, endlessly brimming with creativity. They run marathons and immediately ask what's next and organize the after-party to keep the festivities going. There's never a boring moment with this kind of person around.

That excitement feeds the various hungers that drive Whack-a-Mole Champs. They barter in busyness; it's how they value worth.

The busiest person wins because crazy busy means they're important, right? They volunteer for every project because they don't want to miss out on any opportunity. Compelled to flex their Whack-a-Mole Champ status and garner praise, they unwittingly suck the oxygen out of the room regaling people with how complicated the project was and the fifty-five steps and four sleepless nights it took to resolve and, of course, how they saved the day. Phew!

The question to consider if Whack-a-Mole might be your game of choice is what unmet hunger you are feeding by racing from crisis to crisis? For most champs, it's similar to the need to be needed that drives Caretakers. In their quest to feed that very fundamental (and very normal) hunger, Whack-a-Moles create a reality in which they're the ultimate problem solver and sole provider of answers others must depend on. While they may ace the game, the thrill of their hero status lasts only as long as it takes for the next mole to pop up.

From a Power Gap perspective, Whack-a-Mole Champs are so consumed with clearing the board that they've become desensitized to the damage they are wreaking. Cezar, for instance, had no clue that while problems were indeed getting hammered, so was his team as he careened from one high-stress situation to another with the unpredictability of his namesake carnival game. There was no North Star to his leadership, just the daily whirlwind that yanked his team around. Withholding his strategic thought process and failing to convey a greater sense of purpose were demoralizing to his team, who were forced to do his bidding without the buy-in of ownership—or even partnership, for that matter. Thanks to the distance created by the Power Gap, none of them was willing to tell him they were burning out. Nine months into his role, Cezar started facing a new kind of fire: employees asking for more time off and even leaving to work for the competition.

There will always be another mole, and another, and another. The question is how many whacks does it take before we realize we are winning the game but losing resources and players?

Coaching Consideration: Four Clues You're a Whack-a-Mole

1. You consider crisis management your forte (which it very well may be)
2. You are loath to say no to any opportunity
3. You get bored easily
4. You add things to your to-do list that you've already accomplished, just for the satisfaction of crossing them off

Taming the Whack-a-Mole Urge: Caroline's Story

A mantra I use to stop myself from doing someone else's job if they are not performing is "Don't pick up the work." If an ask or request can wait, I acknowledge it but give it at least a day before taking action. It's often picked up by someone else, and equally often, after a day the ask or request is clearer and easier to resolve. If an urgent ask comes my way from a member of the executive team, and it doesn't have enough information to be actionable, I don't jump in and try to figure it out anymore. I am more comfortable in demanding that others do their job before asking for my help, and the world has yet to collapse.

The Flash

As the oldest of twelve, Mariel was the de facto caretaker for her siblings while her parents worked long days. In the eighth grade, a teacher took notice of her exceptional intellectual abilities and convinced Mariel to set her sights on attending university and becoming a professional in the business world. Mariel was up for the challenge. Waking up at 3 a.m. and studying by a dim light so as not to awaken anyone else, Mariel had one focus: to study. And study hard. With little free time outside her household responsibilities, she worked at warp speed until sunrise to read, study, analyze, and produce work that would dazzle her teachers and earn her the top grades. Her way to bypass the competition was to work harder than anyone around and do it fast, which ultimately placed her first in her high school rankings and earned her a full-ride scholarship to a prestigious university.

Years later, when she had become a vice president of mergers and acquisitions, this racing to get ahead of everyone and everything continued to drive Mariel's actions. While she was on the rise, these traits had catapulted her to the top faster than many others. Once she reached those higher rungs, however, pressure corrupted that hyperefficiency into hoarding all the strategic opportunities for herself.

When she and her team were about to launch a new initiative, Mariel called a meeting to generate ideas. Naturally, she believed she was being efficient when she came to that meeting with a concept draft that was so comprehensive there wasn't much to critique. Her thinking was that she could get this project off the ground faster and in one sitting, which was far more efficient than having to ideate and iterate with the team. While the thirty-minute meeting, like all meetings with Mariel, clocked in at twenty-nine minutes, Mariel resented the lack of feedback or questions from her team, taking it as proof she was the one who had to generate all the ideas. Clearly her team wasn't capable of critical thinking.

Mariel's team may well have been capable of critical thinking. But they, like her, had gotten accustomed to the groove of *Mariel does everything before anyone else can get to it; she clearly doesn't want our input.* Sucking up all the work to herself because she didn't have the patience to let anyone else slow her down meant her team members weren't learning how to think for themselves. As a result, Mariel was piling unnecessary work—and pressure—onto her plate. Just like I did when I was a test manager, she was boxing herself into a corner that left no room for her to upgrade her own skills or career.

Mariel is a workplace version of the Flash, the DC character who employs superhuman speed to solve whatever problem needs solving. Flashes race through their days, voracious in their need to be the heroes of efficiency. They are close cousins of Whack-a-Mole Champs, separated by their methodology. While Whack-a-Moles trade in volume, Flashes trade in velocity. Whack-a-Moles crave more, more, more excitement and the hit of saviorhood, Flashes only have eyes for crossing the finish line first.

I am personally intimately familiar with these behaviors—and I also know the extra work they ironically create. At times I am still guilty of trying to race at breakneck speed *and* be precise and thoughtful. Just the other day, as I was inserting comments into a speech draft for a client, at least fifteen times over the course of an hour I started to type before Word even had time to bring up the comment box. As a result, the first three to four letters of my comment got embedded in the text, causing a red squiggly spelling error line to appear. You'd think I'd learn after the first couple of times, but no! I had to go back to the text and manually delete the extra letters each time, then also had to insert the missing letters into the beginning of the comment box. The microsecond it would have taken me to pause before beginning to type now tripled my efforts and wasted valuable time. We already have enough pressures coming at us; who needs the added self-generated one of avoidable mistakes?

While efficiency is an important quality for managers to have, as Mariel found, there is such a thing as being *too* efficient when it comes at a greater cost to the buy-in and morale of your team. The dust clouds kicked up by Flashes as they race to resolutions and conclusions can obstruct other pathways that might have been far faster, ones that people other than Flashes might see. In their hyperenergized race to the finish line, Flashes often grab on to and run with the first solution that arises, which—surprise!—was generated by them. Masters of the Singular Story, they rarely if ever take a beat to ask "What else might we do in this situation?" and instead zoom ahead, dismissing other voices.

Take Dominic, whose 360 revealed this classic Flash behavior. As one of his direct reports noted, "He does this thing every time we have an all-hands where he fires off an idea and then pretends like he wants our input. He says 'Any thoughts?' but then in basically the same breath says 'No? Okay, great. Let's make it happen!'"

This racing to a conclusion reminds me of hunting dogs who run after the first squirrel that comes along and pounce on it, not realizing they were chasing a paper bag. Dogs don't have the intellectual capacity to step back and ask, *Wait, might a better squirrel be coming? Should I look around and consider alternatives before I take off and chase it down?* But we do. The first solution offered in any situation may not, in fact, be the most strategic move, or even the right one. But if we're so busy chasing down our own first ideas, we're not pausing to notice if someone else has something valuable to contribute that might, in fact, be a better, juicier squirrel.

By shutting down the conversation two seconds after asking if anyone had any thoughts, Dominic essentially communicated he didn't really *want* his team's input. No input meant they had no agency, which in turn meant they were less invested—dare I say interested—in implementing his ideas. As change management expert Daryl R. Connor has noted, the single biggest difference between those who accept change and those who reject it is having some sense of control or say in the matter.

When the drive for breakneck speed takes hold, we can also unknowingly become insensitive to the emotional needs of others. Our compulsion to race to the finish line means we don't stop to think that dropping a quick "We need to talk" to one of our direct reports as we whiz past their office without making eye contact will likely send that person into spasms of worry about what they did wrong or if their job is on the line. Remember, business is *always* personal. We also don't slow down enough to see the utter exhaustion we might be inflicting on our team with our rapid-fire pivots and pace as they scramble to keep up.

Why do some of us race through every interaction, every project? What's the payoff? Our inclination may be to claim ultimate efficiency, but that's only the surface reason. Underneath, some strong hungers are at play. Sometimes it's a fear of missing out (*I must race through this to clear space for the next big thing!*) or the validation of finishing first and best (*I win!*). But most often, the hunger is around control (*If I move lightning fast, no one has time to criticize or thwart my plan*). The drive is to keep a tight grip on the narrative and protect our vision—and hence our relevance—at all costs. It's *my* project, *my* analysis, *my* singular vision, *my* timing and pace. Slowing down means we must let in other ideas and opinions, and that might just mean that ours isn't the single best one or that we don't necessarily get our way. If you ever feel impatient iterating ideas with your team, it's a signal that your hunger for control is running the show.

Coaching Consideration: Six Telltale Signs You're a Flash

1. You walk fast, talk fast, and gesture busily (or like me, listen to audiobooks at 1.5 times the normal speed)

2. You respond to emails and texts within minutes (though admittedly don't always fully answer the question you were asked)

3. You pride yourself on your ability to multitask

4. You frequently interrupt others mid-thought with your flash of an idea

5. Wasted time is your kryptonite (yes, I know I mixed superhero metaphors, but go with it)

6. Patience is not your strong suit

The Straight-A Student

Always the first to raise his hand in response to a teacher's question in grade school, Lance was the consummate Straight-A Student. Driven and off-the-charts brilliant, he set his sights on getting into an Ivy League university and landing a prized job before graduation, both of which he naturally secured. Now a managing director at a consulting firm, Lance is admired by his colleagues for always knowing how to respond to even the most challenging questions from clients.

Like most Straight-A Students, Lance is a perfectionist with sky-high standards. As a result, he demands everyone on his team get his okay on anything before proceeding. Everything—big or small—must go through Lance for quality approval, from the size of the font in the quarterly report to the dollar amount for large initiatives. As Straight-A Students like Lance discover, however, the unyielding hunger for perfection generates pressure that far exceeds the ordinary.

Because all questions lead to Lance and he so tightly holds on to the reins, his team waits for him to respond before they can proceed. Emails pile up with questions about the overall direction so others can make decisions on more specific points, and projects are delayed as his team is left waiting for the bottleneck to clear. "We really need to sit down and do a deep dive so you can take on more of this project" is a frequent refrain from Lance, with a less-than-frequent follow-up. Like throwing a dog a biscuit, Lance's reply to inquiries from his team is always "Good question." This keeps his team trained to ask good questions, waiting for the only-Lance-can-answer-this response and feeling thwarted. By holding the keys to answers and keeping things fuzzy for others, Lance assures himself of top ranking and job security as the Sole Provider of knowledge and wisdom. But he doesn't realize that these actions are causing his top players to exit for stages where they can also shine. Translation: Lance may be succeeding as a star player, but certainly not as a boss.

Straight-A Students like Lance are often indeed the smartest person in the room. They didn't get where they are by luck—their brainpower is the cornerstone of their success. Once again, however, there's a positive and negative dimension at play.

Hard work is the religion of Straight-A Students. It serves as the foundation for their excellence. The negative expression of that all-consuming dedication, however, can be brutal for their well-being as well as for the long-term success of their team. Straight-A Students are the first ones in every morning and the last ones out. They rarely take time off to recharge. They are the ones most likely to fall prey to the Superhero Syndrome you'll read about shortly, in which they override their normal human capacities.

The 24/7 push might make sense when you're working your way up the ladder or building a company, but when you step into next-level roles of authority, your team interprets your approach to work as added pressure. They feel they're expected to sacrifice their own well-being on the altar of straight-A's. You set the pace, the tone, and the expectations. In today's world, the notion of toiling around the clock to the detriment of one's health, family, and work-life balance doesn't fly. As scores of business publications have reported in the wake of the pandemic, Hustle Culture is a relic of the past. It's one thing to project and expect a high work ethic; it's another entirely to suggest your team drive themselves to burnout.

The perfectionism that drives the Straight-A mentality becomes a Pressure Pitfall as the steady demand for superhuman performance grinds down the guardrails that keep you from losing your cool, calm, clearheaded thinking. Perfectionistic behaviors show up in myriad ways, from spending 25 percent of your time correcting the least important details of direct reports' work to extreme anxiety over making mistakes. That anxiety always surfaces, sometimes in surprising ways.

Vanessa, one of my highest-achieving clients, recently contacted me for an emergency session, saying she'd had a full-blown panic attack that morning.

"Oh no," I said. "Okay, let's talk. What happened?"

"Nothing happened, exactly," she responded. "I just have to do a podcast tomorrow, and I've never done one. I'm going to fail, I know it. Should I just cancel?"

I should have known. Vanessa helped launch one of the most innovative health companies in recent years, yet she is among the many who are so driven that the idea of making a mistake is the equivalent of having to declare bankruptcy. The impact of these punishing standards on bosses' team members' mental health is enormous. And as you already know, this in turn hijacks the performance of their team, which hampers results, and the perfection/frustration spiral spins out of control for everyone involved.

While Straight-A Students often know all the answers, their brilliance sometimes causes them to miss the obvious.

Coaching Consideration: Four Giveaways You're a Straight-A Student

1. You're wondering what it will take to ace this quiz
2. High marks and accolades are, for you, better than ice cream on a hot summer day
3. Failure is not an option . . . ever
4. You already know you aced this quiz and are wondering how to win at the rest of this book

---

So what's a Caretaker, Whack-a-Mole Champ, Flash, or Straight-A Student to do now that you know the impact of your Sole Provider tendencies? I won't insult you by simply saying, "delegate." I'm guessing you've tried that before with frustrating results.

That's because even the most successful managers and seasoned executives overlook an important distinction: delegation is not a one-and-done process. It would be great if we could simply provide clear instructions and be instantly relieved of responsibility, freeing up time in our schedules and bandwidth in our brains. But we know it almost never works that way.

Employees are not mind readers. If you give them broad brushstrokes about what you'd like to see and then disappear until the final deliverable is due, likely before a major deadline, there will be errors. Now there's no margin for iteration and adjustment. Naturally, you swoop in and take over, often redoing the entire document and spending Sunday night fuming. We think we're empowering, not micromanaging, when we completely hand off a task to an employee. Instead, we're abdicating, very likely sabotaging the result, and gaslighting our employee.

And your employee? There goes their self-assurance, because they see you have no confidence in them. They feel redundant and micromanaged. As you know, if you frequently swoop in and save the day, your direct reports won't develop the muscles to do better work the next time. This dynamic creates unnecessary pressure for you and demoralizes them as they begin to believe that no matter what they do, their work isn't good enough.

Consider Barbara, the CFO of a public company, who is responsible for running quarterly meetings with shareholders to deliver the earnings report and update on new business developments. Barbara delegates the initial preparation of the script for that meeting to her director of investor relations, Owen. About two weeks before the quarterly meetings, Owen sends Barbara the script for review, and at this point she sends back a version awash with red-lined changes. Barbara expects Owen to learn from her edits and improve the script in the next iteration. Instead, the amount of red remains the same each go-around. In the end, Barbara rewrites most of the script and fumes because Owen "just doesn't get it." Barbara is frustrated by the drain on their time, and Owen feels demoralized by this version of the rock-carrying exercise that appears when the Sage Speak mistake is in play.

As I told Barbara, there is a better way: to treat delegation as a dial, not a switch. By wordlessly handing the draft back to Owen each time and assuming he'll mind-read what she wants through some alchemy of editing osmosis, she is setting them both up for failure. The more viable option is to approach delegation as a dial that must be tuned to the ability and experience level of the person to whom work is being delegated.

Following is the Delegation Dial tool, which you can use as a general practice to tame your Sole Provider tendencies anytime you find yourself in any of these scenarios:

- You are overloaded with tasks others could or should be doing
- You have tried to delegate in the past, and it has not gone well
- You want to mentor a member of your team to take on more responsibility
- Your hesitation around delegation stems from a hunger to be needed, to be relevant, to be in control

The Delegation Dial Tool:
The One Shift Needed for Successful Delegation

Here is a customized approach to delegation, one that yields much greater productivity with far less frustration. At the heart of this strategy is a simple fact: *for delegation to work, it has to come with coaching.*

Put It into Practice

Step One: Identify the knowledge scale

Barbara's initial mistake, like many other delegation-frustrated managers, was not realizing she entered the exchange blinded by the *curse of knowledge*, which we covered in Communication Fault Line #4. As experts, our knowledge is so deeply ingrained that we don't even have to think about it. We assume others are at our level, so we skip over the transfer of our knowledge in digestible pieces.

We can understand this best through the four stages of a learning framework established by management trainer Martin M. Broadwell. The four stages are unconscious incompetence, conscious incompetence, conscious competence, and unconscious competence:

- **Unconscious incompetence.** When we start learning something new, we don't know what we don't know. If you're learning to drive, for instance, this would be the stage at which you've never been behind the wheel of the car and never given much thought to what it would take.

- **Conscious incompetence.** When we learn a bit, we realize what we don't know. We see what doesn't work but don't yet know how to address it. In the driving example, you might do an initial practice run and see all the complexities of operating a car safely that you were never aware of.

- **Conscious competence.** Gradually we take steps to learn how to do this thing. We know we need to turn on the blinker and check the mirror before switching lanes.

- **Unconscious competence.** This is the final stage, in which we've achieved such ease over our subject that we don't have to think about the needed steps—we just perform them automatically. If we've been driving for decades, we likely don't even register turning on the blinker—we just do it. We're unconsciously competent.

To delegate effectively, we must realize that while we're likely operating in the fourth stage, those who work for us may be starting at stage one or two. Owen was at the conscious incompetence stage. He knew what he was doing wasn't working but was unclear what was needed to get him to competence. And unlike driver's education, where he could sign up for training, Owen wasn't sure where to turn to get help, and tried to learn through reading Barbara's edits like he was poring over the rules of the road. Tuning in to where your employee is along these four stages *before* you give them a job allows you to anticipate potential challenges and set them up for success.

How do you tune in to where your employee is on these four stages? You ask them. You assess their level of current competence based on prior work. You provide feedback and see to what degree they're able to adjust. All this will give you the baseline information you need to move to Step Two.

Step Two: Turn the dial to the appropriate notch

Once you establish where your employee is on these four stages of learning, you can turn the dial to the appropriate notch: Do, Tell, Teach, Ask, or Safety Net.

- **Do.** If the person is a complete newbie, do the job and don't ask them to handle it, especially not solo. Instead, have them assist or observe how you do it. In the case of Barbara and Owen, Barbara could have written the draft herself and shown Owen the finished product as she wanted it to read, which he then could use as a model for the next go-around.

- **Tell.** At the next stage, you tell them what they can do to execute. This is where Barbara, as the boss with the larger picture, could begin by stating the desired outcome and the nonnegotiables. She could then share the kind of analysis to include and specifics such as the desired length and tone of the document.

- **Teach.** Once you've communicated the tasks, you teach them the process step by step. Rather than just handing off red-lined drafts to Owen and assuming he would understand what she wanted, Barbara could annotate her edits to give her reasoning behind each comment. Why this part goes at the top, why this phrasing is more appropriate here, why this line is an excellent example of tone? In the next iteration, instead of making revision marks inline, Barbara would only make comments in the margin, such as "Reduce the number of adjectives in this sentence, it comes across as obsequious."

- **Ask.** Only after they've progressed through these first three stages do you *ask*; that is, you coach but no longer instruct them. You ask them what they need from you, if they have hit any roadblocks, gained new insights, or what they're learning as they go along. As Owen's writing skills improved, Barbara would be able to coach him by asking questions like "What's the most important message you want our shareholders to take from this report?" "What other ideas did you have and what made you choose this one?" "What have you learned from the responses to our last shareholder call?"

- **Safety net.** The last step on the Delegation Dial is where most managers start their delegation process (and fail). This last step is only for your most experienced employees, where you offer to be a resource if they need you. Once Owen was nailing the writing process, Barbara could ask him to send her the draft when it was ready and let him know she was there if he had any questions along the way.

No matter how far you've turned the Delegation Dial, for high-stakes outcomes it's useful to set up a series of check-ins to help course correct in little ways early rather than having to execute a hard U-turn at a tight dead end.

After four months, Barbara found she only needed to skim the final draft and Owen was self-sufficient. If you're wondering whether you have time to shepherd processes like this for four months, consider that Barbara had been red-lining Owen's drafts for a year with no improvement. The Delegation Dial puts to good use the business adage of "go slow to go fast."

Speaking of going slow, you must turn the Delegation Dial slowly. My client Tim's wife had hip surgery, after which she could not bear any weight on it for twelve weeks. Once she could walk a bit, I asked Tim how she was doing, and he replied that she'd healed to the point of dangerously overdoing things. The same happens with the Delegation Dial. Once we set our mind to handing off tasks and have someone to delegate to, we're as desperate for them to take over as Tim's wife was to get back to the gym. Be conscious of sticking to the five stages of the Delegation Dial rather than turning the knob too soon and dangerously overdoing it, leading to disappointment for you and disempowerment for your staff.

 Pro Tip: Address the Delegation *"yeah, buts"* Head-On

Are your *"yeah, buts"* raging? You're not alone. Perhaps more than any other tool, the Delegation Dial stirs up a lot of objections. Below are the five most common *"yeah, buts"* I hear and strategies to shift them into *"yes, ands."*

Objection: It'll take too long
Strategy: . . . and track how long it takes you now to repeatedly undo and redo tasks you've delegated. Yes, it might take more time up front, and that investment pays off when you no longer have to revise your employees' work.

Objection: We could drop the ball on an important project
Strategy: . . . and so you need to start small and turn the dial slowly. Don't start by delegating a presentation to the board. We don't teach our kids to ride bikes on the freeway, we do it in a cul-de-sac with training wheels.

Objection: They lack attention to detail
Strategy: . . . and instead of picking up the details, use the Tell and Teach notches on the Delegation Dial until your employee tunes into what matters. Give them a list of common mistakes.

Objection: They're too slow
Strategy: . . . and check to make sure you're not operating on "manager time" from the other side of the Power Gap, where you're so far removed from the task or so clear on it yourself (the curse of

knowledge) that you don't have realistic time expectations. Ask your direct reports for a time frame they think is reasonable.

Objection: They don't think critically enough

Strategy: . . . and this can be taught. Enhance team members' critical thinking skills by asking powerful coaching questions like "On launch day, how will our competitors celebrate because we had a blind spot?" or "What's common across the last seven customer complaints?"

Delegation Dial in Action: Kai's Story

Before I started employing the Delegation Dial, I had two modes of managing work tasks: "do it yourself" and "assign and see/hope for the best." I preferred the "do it yourself" route because the vision for the outcome of the meeting was typically clear in my mind, I had all the relevant context, and I could do it faster than someone else on the team. "Assign and see/hope" felt more like a gamble and was significantly less comfortable for me. I wondered why someone else should take this on if I was perfectly capable of doing it, and I worried about burdening my team and their ability to deliver what I was expecting.

The first mode created an untenably long to-do list, made me a bottleneck for progress, and created the conditions for my own burnout. The second one had inconsistent results; sometimes the deliverable was very successful and increased my confidence in the team member. Other times it failed to meet my vision and had the opposite impact of my confidence in that employee—and increased my reluctance to delegate.

In one instance, I assigned a task to a direct report whom I consider to be more of an expert than me on the topic. I expected they would have enough context to create an upcoming presentation without a more detailed up-front conversation. When it came time to review a draft of the slides, I realized I had not provided enough context and direction (examples, objectives, etc.). I had to revise their work, which undercut their confidence and created late-night work for me.

I knew I had to adjust my approach and move away from a one-size-fits-all framework. Using the Delegation Dial as a diagnostic tool helped me determine the right level of context, background, and direction needed in a particular instance. With some of my more experienced team members, the style of delegation would call for more guiding and coaching tactics, versus dictation of the deliverable, which I now reserve for select instances.

For example, when I was helping a team member prepare for a challenging meeting with a key internal partner, I asked them to think about the partner's concerns and what a successful outcome of the conversation would be. In my old way of working, I would have listed out the agenda items and likely led the meeting myself. In this case, the team member used my questions to create an agenda and led the conversation to a successful outcome. Today, this team member has increased confidence in their ability to effectively influence and manage challenges.

I wouldn't say I have mastered applying the Delegation Dial, but I have seen real improvement over the past few months and expect continued progress and positive impact for my team and me.

 Delegation Dial Micro Habits

- Once a day, ask a coaching question instead of providing a prescriptive direction
- Stop what you're doing and ask yourself if someone else could and should do this task instead

CHAPTER TWELVE

Get Unstuck from the Minutiae Web

If your immediate reaction to this chapter title is anything along the lines of "Sabina, you have no *idea*," you're in the right place. I can assure you of three things:

1. I get you
2. You are far from alone
3. There *is* a way out from under

To free you from the daily crush of minutiae, we first have to back up and get a read on how you landed there in the first place. How did you come to get buried under thousands of details and tasks that make work feel stifling, overwhelming, demoralizing, and more? Even more importantly, why?

Ezra is a great case study in the psychology behind the lure of the minutiae web. He is the chief people officer for a medical supply manufacturer. He rose up the ranks through HR to his current C-suite role in which he oversees multiple human resource divisions within this global organization. Like many executives on the "people" side of corporations during the pandemic, Ezra found navigating the intricacies of COVID testing and remote work highly complex. In fact, I convened a small group of my chief people officer clients to meet biweekly as they took on new responsibilities for which they dubbed themselves chief COVID officers. This was uncharted territory for everyone, and their skills had to level up at previously unexperienced speeds to meet the rapidly changing landscape. This was especially true for Ezra given that his company was on the front lines of supplies needed by hospitals, so we bumped our sessions up from biweekly to weekly to help him respond to the onslaught of challenges he faced daily.

In one of our sessions, Ezra made a passing reference to still not having worked out the height of the COVID-testing protecting screens for the offices. Knowing Ezra as I do, I realized the fact that he tried to slip this in and then quickly move on meant that he both wanted me to catch it and was also kind of hoping I didn't. Naturally, I called him out on it.

"Wait, I missed that," I said. "What is it that you're trying to work out?"

"Oh, we're trying to establish the right height of medical privacy screens in the testing area. Each person is going to be rapid-tested in the morning before they come into the office," he said. "If we go with the 177-centimeter height, I am concerned people won't feel like it's private enough, but the 223-centimeter ones will take an extra two weeks to arrive and block the windows, and it might feel claustrophobic."

All valid concerns . . . for a human resources director. But for a chief people officer during a global pandemic, a detail like the centimeter height of a COVID-testing screen was about as important as removing a pebble from your shoe when you're running from a tsunami.

A lot of times, like Ezra, we inflate the importance of work that isn't central to our bigger goals. Yes, your calendar is likely packed with back-to-back meetings. Yes, the daily onslaught of questions, demands, problems, tasks, requests is vast. Yes, there is less bandwidth than is needed to complete everything on your to-do list, and we are living in a world where we have to do more with fewer resources. I get it, believe me. But as I tell my clients, the real challenge isn't figuring out how to tackle what's on that to-do list; it's examining how it got on there in the first place. Where are you picking out pebbles from your shoe when your focus should be on outrunning the tsunami?

As burdensome as being mired in the minutiae can feel at times, it does keep us safely in our comfort zone. This is the "automating" part of the response to pressure, otherwise known as reverting to what's familiar. Leaving our comfort zone always comes with risk. Remember, under pressure all synapses fire to keep us safe from danger. Staying "safe" usually translates to holding on to the tasks of your former role, like Ezra grasping on to a decision that easily could have been made by one of his direct reports. Up until that point, Ezra had always been the number two to a world-class manager. The former CPO always took his suggestions, but Ezra wasn't the one making the ultimate call. Suddenly, he was in a high-pressure position where his mistakes could lead his team and company down a rabbit hole. He could make decisions that would anger people. Former prime minister of the UK Tony Blair once said, "When you decide, you divide." With a strong hunger to be liked, Ezra was uncomfortable knowing that there would always be someone who was unhappy with whatever call he made.

Now that it was just him out there without anyone to hide behind, Ezra slid back into who he had been instead of who he was meant to grow into. To avoid the discomfort, he continued the tasks he was used to doing rather than focusing on the strategic, bigger-picture work he was meant to do. Unknowingly guided by that prehistoric survival brain, many managers make this backward-looking choice without realizing (a) that they are doing so, (b) why they are doing so, and (c) that doing so is the exact opposite of what their next-level role requires of them.

The bigger payoff out here in the non-Pleistocene era is that you have every excuse in the book for not being able to step out of the muck to do the bigger-picture strategizing. The threat isn't a tiger but rather a fear that even some of the world's most innovative thought leaders are stalked by during the dead of the night: *What if I actually don't have what it takes to think strategically? What if the ideas I come up with mean I need to confront hard truths and make big changes that I'd rather not have to contend with? What if my ideas don't work and I fail?*

The truth is anyone can think strategically if they create the time and space for it. The question is, are you willing to step away from the protective shield of the minutiae and go there? Are you willing to challenge yourself to ask bigger-picture questions, to explore the outer edges of your strategic capacities? Even more, are you willing to put into action what you dream up in that cleared space?

The muck of minutiae brings all our Sole Provider behaviors to the fore. This swampy terrain awakens the "I got you, don't worry" instincts of the Caretaker, who swoops in to handle everyone's to-do list on top of their own. Straight-A Students are lured in by the appeal of micromanaging every detail to perfection. Flashes get to check off their to-do lists first—over and over. And perhaps most pointedly, Whack-a-Moles get to wade in the bottomless busyness they crave.

Busyness is a fabulous excuse to hide behind. When I was on the board of a nonprofit agency, one of the other board members volunteered to use her resources to generate funding for a needed upgrade to the agency's IT systems. This woman was a whirlwind of energy with extensive contacts, so it seemed like the ideal scenario. True to form for this behavior type, however, she was so stuck in her busyness that she never followed through. At every board meeting, I braced myself because I knew I was about to get hit with the torrent of "Oh my gosh I've just been so *busy* . . . are you as *busy* as I am these days? We're just so *busy!*"

This woman was a classic example of how conveniently the busyness of minutiae gets us off the hook. It's a difficult thing to admit that being mired in busy is a choice—which we often avoid because it means we have to face an unmet hunger of being seen as indispensable. My client Rose Marie has four kids, a husband, and a huge job as a professor and researcher. She brings all the rigor of her professional life home with her. Recently as she was lamenting her overloaded plate, she said, "It's just a lot. I have to work a full day, then come home, make dinner, clean up, and then do my evening work."

"Whoa," I said. "Where's the family in all this? Can't they at least help with cleaning up?"

"Oh, they don't load the dishwasher right," she said. "So I have to do it. The kitchen has to be 100 percent clean before I go to bed, so I just get it done."

The issue at hand wasn't Rose Marie's to-do list but her need for control. What would happen if the kitchen *wasn't* 100 percent spotless before bedtime? What would it mean for her if she really learned to delegate the right way and doled out vitamins rather than painkillers for her dishwasher-compromised family members? What might shift if she recognized she was playing the rescuer in the Drama Triangle? Remember, we are always complicit in some way in our circumstances. The choice comes down to your willingness to see where you are perpetuating the minutiae mire and then—and this part is key—being willing to act differently with that knowledge.

Your role as the boss is to be the chef, not a line cook. Your work is not to julienne every vegetable but to create a new recipe. The mise en place work of organizing your ingredients is where you start, but then you need to leave the work of preparing the meal in the hands of others because that's where and when your hands-on work ends and you're freed up to create the next big thing. Too many don't leave the stove because they believe the Sole Provider stories they tell themselves, that no one can do it the way they can, as fast as they can, as thoroughly as they can. Underneath of course is fear of our own corporate mortality. *If I don't do this, who am I? What's my value? If I give this up, what then? Am I really worthy of ascending to the next level? Do I even want to?* There is *so* much justifying around this delegating piece. One of the five questions I ask when I first take someone on is, "To what degree do you delegate?" Almost every one of them says, "I delegate well when I trust someone." They haven't considered how they've established and built trust with their team, so the team can do something beyond what they've already been doing.

You know the data, you know the competition, you likely have the institutional knowledge. The higher up you go, the more likely you are to chase details that you don't need to anymore (ahem, the height of the COVID-testing screen). It's not that details don't matter, it's that they take up time and space you need for something else. Do you really need to go three levels deep into a spreadsheet? If your answer is yes, it signals that two forces are at play: first, you're avoiding letting go of your past role and stepping into the new one, and second, you don't trust your team to be on top of those details. When it's the latter, you can blame them all you want and you might be right, but remember, you as the boss are always complicit in some way. It's just more convenient to make ourselves the victim (or rescuer) rather than the villain in our own story. Being the boss means being responsible and taking accountability, not by doing it all ourselves but by being the one who teaches the team and doles out growth-inducing vitamins instead of temporary-fix painkillers.

Being mired in minutiae is not a permanent state of being. The Blank Space tool outlined below is a powerful means to climb out of the muck weighing you down, renew your ability to think clearly and strategically, and restore your creativity—not to mention your sense of well-being.

Coaching Consideration:

What would you be freed up to do (or, conversely, have to face) if your calendar was cleared of minutiae?

Blank Space: Make Room for What Really Matters

Use this tool when you experience any of these telltale signs of being mired in minutiae:

- **You feel consistently pressed for time or overwhelmed**
- **You are unable to step back from the daily details to see the bigger picture**
- **You are having trouble thinking clearly**

- You experience symptoms of burnout: sleeplessness, exhaustion (physical, mental, or emotional), lack of interest or joy in your work, a feeling of incompetence or uselessness, easily agitated, difficulty paying attention, relying on comfort vices like drinking or food to self-soothe

Our focus on minutiae not only keeps us stuck in details that don't matter or that others are capable of handling, but blocks out our bigger ideas. We have more ideas than we give ourselves credit for. We know more than we realize. We just need to provide space for those ideas to come out.

A wealth of scientific research shows our best thinking comes when we give our brains a chance to quiet down. Creativity peaks when the portion of our brains responsible for executive functioning—meaning decision-making, analyzing, and planning—is on pause. The portion of the brain responsible for learning and memory regenerates with new cells when afforded blocks of silence. Insights appear spontaneously when we shift the brain to an inward focus. This is why we tend to have our best aha moments while idly cruising down the highway, in the shower, running, or walking the dog.

It was only when I stopped go, go, going long enough to allow my inner radar to recalibrate in real time that I hit upon the stunning realization all those years ago that I didn't *want* to progress to the vice president role that was within my grasp. From time to time, I ponder how my life would be different if I hadn't given myself that space for my true professional desires to bubble up. I might have woken up one day wondering why I felt so miserable in a big, cushy job as corporate VP.

Space to just be is more important than many managers realize. When you occupy the authority role, you act as a metronome, setting the cadence for the rest of your team. To reset our metronome and create new ways of tackling challenges, we need to eliminate noise and create space to think. I call this *Blank Space*. When we read a book and look at the words on the page, we can make out distinct words and make sense of the words, sentences, and paragraphs because there is also Blank Space in between each letter, word, sentence, paragraph, and in the margins. Without this space, the letters would be a senseless jumble of ink. And so it is with our time. Blank Space allows us to clearly read the writing in our minds. We don't need a lot of Blank Space, just enough to make sense of what we're doing and whether we're focused on the right things.

Perhaps more than any other tool, Blank Space demands attention to the Cost vs. Benefit Equation. The instant I tell my busiest clients that they need to step away from the busyness even briefly, the *"yeah, buts"* start raging with the force of a Gulf Coast hurricane. "You're insane, Sabina, I barely have time to see my kids let alone take time to myself . . . ," "Ha, if only I had the luxury of stepping away, but if I do, everything will fall apart . . . ," "I have way too much to do to give up any time . . ." Our hungers sound the sirens of alarm as the habits we've cultivated to keep them sated feel vulnerable to attack. The loss of time or of the strong hold we have (or think we have) on our workload can feel threatening.

And yet, you're here reading this book because you're looking to grow. You already know what staying the course yields. The question is, what are you missing out on that might catapult you way beyond where you currently are?

Yes, you'll be giving up a bit of work time to carve out Blank Space. But as you'll see in the stories in the section below, it's an expenditure that pays for itself.

Put It into Practice

Over the years, my clients and I have experimented with the duration of Blank Space and the tools that help sustain it and create transformational results. The client stories below reveal the results of those experiments that will help you establish a Blank Space practice.

Plan for it like you would any other important commitment

Blocking and protecting space to be is the first victory. To carve out your weekly Blank Space sanctuary, book two hours back-to-back whenever possible. I recommend two hours because this is the chunk of time it takes for our to-do list and other quotidian thoughts to quiet down, and to flesh out bigger ideas.

Here is what my client Peter, a marketing manager for a franchising operation in the food industry, said about booking Blank Space:

> The most important key for me is reviewing my calendar in two-week increments and working with my admin to formally block time on my agenda. We usually choose two-hour chunks on Wednesdays or Thursdays. There's no particular reason for that timing; it just seems to work best. I try not to get stressed if we're not able to block time for each week. We seem to be able to get time on the calendar at least every other week, and there have been good stretches when I am able to string a few weeks together. It really helps that my admin is so good at calendar management. Plus, she's respectful of this time and doesn't try to coerce me into giving it back for the inevitable third-party "urgent" requests for my time.

Do nothing (or at least close to nothing)

The next question is, what exactly do we do during Blank Space? In its purest form, we do nothing; we just sit or walk. Here is what Peter shared regarding his "do nothing" time:

> For me, this time truly has to be distraction-free. The way I get "undistracted" is to go offline and, usually, leave the office. At first, I thought that being online would be okay, since there is so much good, rich content on the web that can stretch one's mind, but I've found that that doesn't work for me—there are just too many job-related pop-ups that either intrude or to which I too easily stray,

like email (personal as well as corporate), company news, the stock market, and the regular news. Others might find many of those topics perfectly acceptable for their own Blank Space time, but they don't work for me.

My Blank Space time is most effective when I spend it doing 100 percent unstructured thinking outdoors, preferably in nature. Forests, mountains, lakes, rivers, streams all work. Driving in nature is good, walking is even better. Human-made places are okay, too, especially if I have no investment or emotional attachment to them, like new parts of Seattle that I haven't walked before. (Nine times out of ten, when I leave the office and get into my truck, I have no idea where I'm going to go.) When I do this, I try not to dwell on any particular issue. I just try to be. I observe. I feel. I sense. I breathe. I see. Somehow this washes me. It's literally like my brain is being cleansed—sometimes it's an actual physical sensation that I feel in my head, as though someone were gently wiping away all the static clinging to my brain.

If this kind of empty wandering feels too challenging, give yourself something mindless to do. Bring a sketchpad and colored pencils and doodle. Tinker with a set of building blocks or do any easy activity that engages your hands. Interestingly, menial work like washing dishes is among the best choices for Blank Space. In his novel *Tress of the Emerald Sea*, author Brandon Sanderson writes, "That is one of the great mistakes people make: assuming that someone who does menial work does not like thinking. Physical labor is great for the mind, as it leaves all kinds of time to consider the world. Other work, like accounting or scribing, demands little of the body—but siphons energy from the mind. If you wish to become a storyteller, here is a hint: sell your labor, but not your mind. Give me ten hours a day scrubbing a deck, and oh the stories I could imagine. Give me ten hours adding sums, and all you'll have me imagining at the end is a warm bed and a thought-free evening."

Whether you choose to do origami, wash windows, or go for a walk, the key is to find Blank Space settings that work best for you. While Peter favors alone time in nature with unstructured thinking, he occasionally chooses another route:

> The other plan usually involves a book I've been exploring and which I feel has the potential to teach me new thinking. I'll find a quiet place in a park or next to a lake, and I'll sit and read for a couple of hours. The cleansing feeling is not nearly as good when I'm reading as when I'm just thinking. Taking in new information, even if it's scintillating, still seems to be some kind of work that doesn't allow the same sense of mental freedom leading to washing that comes from unstructured thinking. But if the content is good enough, the positive effects are still great. My moments of epiphany are fewer and farther between while reading, versus only thinking, but they still come—it's just someone else's voice they come through, not so much my own.

Be patient with "monkey mind"

For many, the early stages of practicing Blank Space can feel a little unsettling. Any practitioner of meditation can tell you that the first few minutes of doing nothing are the hardest because thoughts ricochet around our minds. *I forgot to do this . . . I have to tell them to do that . . . Did I leave the coffeepot turned on?* The unofficial term for this is "monkey mind," as in our thoughts swinging from branch to branch, cackling and screeching for attention. It takes patience to sit through those first few minutes or, as a newbie to Blank Space, the first hour, but once you let them flail around wildly for a bit, the monkeys quiet down.

Choose a theme

For some clients, giving their Blank Space an umbrella theme proves helpful. You can choose a big topic as your theme each week, like one of those hairy subjects that you keep pushing off because it can't be handled in the fifteen minutes in between meetings, or a more general one, like "my team." Hold the theme loosely and don't direct your thoughts—just let them wander and jot down whatever comes up. Your brain might start firing up insights, or at the very least, you'll return with a well-rested brain that then performs on higher octane. You can also keep a running list of thoughts that arise in these Blank Space sessions, which over time may connect to form a pattern. This happened for Letitia, an advertising sales manager. One day, she looked over her list and spotted a gap in the firm's Asia market. She wrote a memo to the board, was promoted two levels, and asked to lead the company's Asia strategy.

On the other hand, here's what Peter noted about his Blank Space experience:

> When I first began doing the Blank Space exercise, I expected or hoped for brilliant flashes of insight specific to my current day job. That has never really happened. Instead, what I've experienced is a gradual, deeper, and quite beautiful, better understanding of who I am and what I can bring to society (within but not limited to the workplace) as I've listened to my own voice. My voice has always been there, but I couldn't hear it through all the noise I carried with me as I rushed from one meeting to the next, from one email to the next, from one office swordfight to the next, from one worry to the next. I realize now there's a lot to be said for keeping still, remembering that you are you.

 Blank Space Micro Habit

Once a day, step away from all devices, reading, and conversation for thirty seconds. Stare off into the distance, walk up and down the front stairs, or simply close your eyes.

Acknowledge emotional resistance

The habit of busyness can be a hard one to break. Ignoring the resistance to stepping away from work is futile; guilt is a potent emotion. The key is to acknowledge the pull of the status quo where "busy = important" and then *do the Blank Space exercise anyway*.

Here is Peter's thinking:

There is guilt associated with taking Blank Space, although that emotion is most present just as my scheduled time approaches and I contemplate leaving work. It intensifies when I shut down my computer and head for the elevator. It's especially bad as I run into colleagues on my way down twelve floors to the parking garage. I imagine that they notice that I'm going someplace, with no professional tool in hand, and must think that I'm going out to play hooky. In fact, I am. [Grin.] I think of my direct reports and wonder what they would think if they knew that their boss was walking out the door when they—as I imagine—are all working hard. I worry that they would disrespect me or think that I'm lazy.

When I return from my Blank Space time, I realize how silly it was to feel guilty because what I've just experienced has made me a better, more complete human being who brings back to the workplace an important remembrance of who I am and a renewed determination to live up to that ideal.

 Pro Tip: Overcome the Six Common Obstacles to Blank Space

Obstacle: Important meetings hijack my blank space
Strategy: Find a slot that's less popular for meetings, such as earlier/later in the day or Friday afternoons.

Obstacle: Others book time over my slot
Strategy: Name it something important sounding like "strategic

planning" so others peeking at your calendar don't squat in that spot.

Obstacle: My mind is taken over by my to-do list
Strategy: Book some *doing* time before this *being* time so you don't give it up to your to-do list. For example, if you're going to do blank space on Friday from 10 a.m. to noon, book some time to clean up your inbox and your task list from 3 to 5 p.m. on Thursday.

Obstacle: I get distracted by notifications
Strategy: Eliminate noise. Be offline. No connectivity, no devices, no conversations, no reading. Promising yourself that "you're just researching" will soon mean you're on a YouTube binge instead.

Obstacle: People interrupt me
Strategy: Place matters. You're less likely to get interrupted if you're away from work and possibly even home. Client examples: booking a conference room in another building; a walk in the park; hammock in the yard; a local coffee shop. One person's goal was to test every pie shop in his city—he'd order two pies and park himself for two hours in a new café each week.

Blank Space in Action: Satej's Story

Two years ago, I seemed to be in constant firefighting mode, juggling my schedule and my deliverables. It was a very reactive point in my career, and I was not able to put together a meaningful long-term plan for the desired state of my business. The other negative impact of running my business this way was that my work spilled over into my personal life. I used to get in early, work till six, come home and be with my wife and kids for a couple of hours, then once they were in bed, I would log back in and work until midnight or later. I'd wake up the next morning and start the cycle again. My family suffered, and my work was not as impactful as it could have been.

About this time, I started working with Sabina, and she suggested the Blank Space approach. At first, I was reluctant—sorry, Sabina, I just could not imagine sitting in a room with no phone and no laptop for three to four hours and being expected to have ideas and creativity flow about my business. I just did not think I could do it. At first it did not work for me—I was too caught up in my "lost" time away from laptop to completely unplug.

However, I was determined to make it work, and sure enough, over time it became easier to unplug for long periods of time. The results happened almost immediately, which gave me some great positive reinforcement to continue. My ideas began to flow once again, and the quality of work improved. The other benefit was my home life improved as well. I almost never look at a work device while I'm at home, and my family interactions are much better now.

Everybody is different, but I approach my Blank Space time with a couple of different methods and ground rules. My Blank Space time is blocked on my calendar every week, and my manager and team members are aware of this time and have come to respect it over the last two years. Other than a family obligation or some other critical extenuating circumstance, I let no obligation conflict with this time. Those exceptions maybe happen a couple of times a year now and that's it. Setting this firm boundary is critical to success with Blank Space work.

I do two forms of the Blank Space. I either lock myself in a conference room in a building different than my usual office, or I take it outside. I can get out on my bike for a two- to three-hour ride, and I tend to come up with my most creative ideas while I'm thinking on the bike. I never listen to music when I'm working out. Just me, my bike, and my thoughts. This works well for me. And I get feedback from my team members that I'm more focused and relaxed after

I have spent time in that state, and I'm a better leader and more attuned to the subtle things I may have missed in the past. I can see the whole picture, and when I look at my peers who have not adopted this approach, I see myself two years ago running around frantic and not being the leader I was capable of being.

CHAPTER THIRTEEN

Superhero Syndrome

"I must do it all," says the Sole Provider.

The Superhero, not to be outdone, replies, "Oh, but I *can* do it all."

Infallible. Able to exist on four hours of sleep, caffeine, and Power Bars. Shows up remotely for work when they have the flu. Makes it clear to their friends and family that work comes first, either in words or actions. Leaves for vacation (if they take any) with their laptop in hand and emails to all in their universe letting them know they are fully reachable at any time while away. We all know the type. Maybe we even are the type.

Superheroes, say hello to your customized Pressure Pitfall. Can you do it all? Probably. Is that serving you as a manager? You already know the answer.

Those with Superhero Syndrome may be aware of the triggers that set them off when pressure mounts, but they completely override them. Remember Benita, whose staff was threatening to walk out on her because they were so unhappy? Even though Benita was initially unaware of the *effect* of her behaviors, she did know her own tendencies. She knew Wednesdays were a particularly stressful day, as that was the day her weekly column for an industry publication was due. Yet she insisted that was a "nonissue" and scheduled important meetings on Wednesdays, all of which almost always went badly. It was only when we started to track many of the incidents that arose in her 360 to Wednesdays that she could see the correlation.

My point is that even if you think you're powering through, you're not. Burnout and frayed emotional capacities have ways of leaking past your psyche and into your physical space. If you need proof of that, ask the people closest to you in your life—your partner, your kids, your friends. They'll give it to you straight. Unmanaged pressure dumps us into a pitfall of frayed tempers where circumstances seem more dire and out of control. Like the Hulk, your best traits transmute into your worst.

My client Maya is an Energizer Bunny type who gets more done before 7 a.m. than many do in an entire day. However, whenever she is overly sleep-deprived, that energy tips into frantic and she becomes sloppy on details and abrasive in her communication. One comment from her 360 read, "When Maya is tired and stressed, she becomes curt and harder to talk to. She goes into a mode where she talks over people or dismisses their point with an actual eye roll. A lot of people around here try to avoid her on those days." I routinely remind her she doesn't do well when she's exhausted and that trading off a few hours of sleep for crossing ten more things off her to-do list would generate far greater returns.

When you're in a power role, self-care is not something you need to make time for outside your job; rather it is *part* of your job. I'd go so far as to say it's Priority #1 in your job. Your mental, physical, and emotional well-being is what fuels your capacity to lead and manage your team to success. If your inner machinery is well oiled, you'll run at maximum efficiency. If it's faulty or running on fumes, your creativity, job satisfaction, and results will be, too—and not just yours but those of your team who depend on you.

The job of being boss is hard—harder than most of us can reasonably be expected to survive, let alone thrive in. Just about every manager I work with has come to understand they need to invest in their self-care heavily if they aim to thrive. The research on the link between self-care and success is indisputable. In their work on the "corporate athlete," based on exercise science, performance psychologist Jim Loehr and CEO Tony Schwartz make the point that what gets in the way of excelling and winning is not stress, but the absence of recovery. They point out that the average professional athlete spends most of their time training and only a fraction competing, whereas the typical executive devotes little if any time to training and yet is called on to perform for upward of twelve hours per day.

I think you get the point here. Allotting time for recovery as much as for doing is a key for getting out of chaos and into higher and better thinking. Yes, things happen at work that demand your time and attention, absolutely. But the crucial question is, how can those things be tended to without sacrificing your own needs?

The answer is by assessing what you are choosing, hour by hour, day by day.

People often privilege their work busyness over anything that has to do with themselves, until they hit a wall. Then and only then do they start to prioritize even their most basic self-care. I've lost count of the number of people I've worked with who have IBS, high blood pressure, strained marriages, fractured relationships with their kids, and more, all in the name of "It's my job . . . I have no choice."

I used to think that way, too. As I mentioned earlier, the person most likely to suffer from Superhero Syndrome is a Straight-A Student—a personality type I know well, being one myself. My whole life I have been driven by a need to be the smartest person in the room, to never fail, to be valued for my perfect performance, for always knowing the answer, for being the best. This mythology in my family started when I was two years old. My parents brought me to the zoo and were in awe because I could name all the animals, while my cousin of the same age could say only "mama" and "balloon." I heard them bragging about this again and again, breeding a sense of superiority into me. As I got older, this superiority translated into unassailability. I was impervious to challenges, unable to be brought down by even the most demanding situation. I was so obsessed with scoring high on my exams that I once accidentally set my hair on fire while studying by candlelight during a power failure and noticed only when I smelled an acrid burning odor. In my early adult work life, I would power through anything and everything in my sixteen-hour workdays, including allotting myself one fifteen-minute ugly cry in my office the day after my dad died and then powering on until I boarded a plane back to India to manage his affairs.

As a manager, I'd spend my days in constant crisis response mode, often feeling like an outfield catcher racing back and forth to field all the questions and issues batted my way. I was 100 percent convinced this was how it had to be. That is, until my nervous system revolted with crippling vertigo, and I had to slow things down—way down. I had many fears about how things would turn out (not well) and what others would think of me (not highly) if I cut back on work. But much like the Superhero lament about not having a choice, this time I really didn't. Only now, prioritizing my well-being had become nonnegotiable. It was time to trade in my Superhero cape and cure myself of the workaholism bred by perfection.

To make the shift, I assessed what was taking up time and what I was saying yes to. For example, my meetings were spread across the week to accommodate various clients' schedules, which meant I essentially never had a day off. I chose to block out every Tuesday as a meeting-free weekday. Not only did I not schedule meetings on Tuesdays, I communicated to my clients' assistants that I was available every day of the week except for Tuesdays. Setting a clear boundary made it clear to others what worked and reduced the number of back-and-forth calendar negotiations with each new request.

Guess what? Not only did no one fire me; no one really seemed to mind at all.

The next challenge was upholding the value of being responsive—a point of pride for me—without compromising rest time. Instead of jumping in to field every request, I committed to pause and determine what was really a pressing need that necessitated immediate attention. For instance, a client would ask, "Sabina, I just gave this talk on CNN, would you please review it and give me feedback because I want to be better prepared for my next media interview?" Instead of yet again putting off a trip to the gym to get to that review immediately, I would ask what their timeline was. Nine times out of ten, their timeline was far longer, two to three times longer, than I had anticipated.

I also had to learn probably the hardest aspect of boundary setting: saying no. Of course, I wanted to fly to Dubai to give that speech . . . or run the off-site for my client and his team in Mexico . . . or take on an endless roster of fascinating coaching clients. Who wouldn't? With each opportunity, however, I had to ask myself: *If I choose to say yes to this, what am I giving up? What might be compromised?* Time and bandwidth are finite resources, so it is *always* a trade-off. Yes, even for the most infallible of self-appointed Superheroes.

In each of these cases, instead of going into my default mode of just taking on the work or saying yes, I asked myself what I needed to do to set boundaries, check other people's time expectations, and determine the urgency of a task. As a result, not only did I get more sleep, more exercise, and stave off unnecessary vertigo attacks, but I got more done because I was better rested and therefore more efficient during my waking hours. To this day, I get more quality work accomplished in less time by operating this way. I've learned that sustaining my own well-being is the foundation to keeping myself focused.

As you already know from Part Two, if you want to be a strong, confident, effective boss, you need to first and foremost be a strong, confident, and effective boss of *you*—and that includes actively taking control of your time and your well-being. Not "someday" or "when I have time," but now.

Taking care of yourself usually consists of commonsense basics—sleep, exercise, nutrition, downtime to let your adrenal system settle, cultivating gratitude, and spending time with loved ones. It doesn't matter if it's a meditation app, running three miles a day, time in nature, reading, or lying on the couch with your dog—you are smart, you know what does it for you. What matters is that you *do* the thing. The Time Portfolio tool will show you how to turn your fantasy of *I'll get to self-care one of these days* into a reality you can step into today and sustain for the long haul.

Self-care, after all, is what gives us genuine Superhero strength.

The Time Portfolio: Reclaim Your Valuable Hours

Use this tool to get a handle on how you allocate the finite hours in the day, specifically when:

- **Your calendar feels out of control**
- **You say yes when you really would prefer to say no**
- **You end your days frustrated by all the items you did not cross off your to-do list**
- **You have no time for big-picture strategizing**
- **Your personal relationships and/or health are suffering**

"I don't have enough time."

How many times have you thought this? I've lost count myself of how many clients have lamented a shortage of time to do all the things they need to get done.

The problem, however, isn't a lack of time. It's a lack of fidelity.

In my leadership workshops, I often ask, "How many of you are paid to innovate?" Nearly every hand in the room goes up.

Then I ask, "How many of you have time on your calendar to inno-vate?" No more than one or two hands out of twenty-four go up.

That's low fidelity. Is your calendar faithful to what you say you value?

A lot of magical thinking goes on when it comes to time. We indulge in it when we overestimate how much we can get done in two hours (the Time Fairy), when we are convinced *I'll stick to my timetable* this *time* (the Pixie Dust Fix), and when we put our faith in *Somehow it will all get done and the magical elves will help me* (the Overnight Elves).

I don't know about you, but I'm definitely a time fantasizer. If I find a thirty-minute hole in my day, I mentally stuff it with twenty things that would take five times as much time as I'm imagining. In his comedy special *Baby J*, actor and comedian John Mulaney tells a story about the night of his intervention. Mulaney shares how he booked a hair-cut at 9 p.m.—the precise time he promised he'd arrive at his friend's apartment—and jokes he was *absolutely sure* he could make both of those work. Mulaney freely admits he was heavily under the influence of prescription drugs at the time, but many of us are under a similar blurring influence of our own magical thinking.

The Stories We Tell Ourselves About Time

1. This is an especially busy time of year, so I need to just do this for my team to help get them through
2. If I handle the situation, my team will follow my example and figure out how to tackle something similar next time on their own
3. I'll say yes this once because they won't like me/won't ask me again if I don't
4. How long can this possibly take?

Even if we were to magically double the time we have in a week, many of us would still have the same problem of being time-starved and overwhelmed because of our habitual magical thinking. We are all veteran storytellers regarding how much time it takes to do things and what we can get done.

We can't bend the rules of time and space, but we can increase our intentionality in how we invest the time we do have. Time is our most precious asset, not money. We create portfolios to manage our money—why not create one for our time? For your money, you scope out what you have, how much risk you want to take, your future goals, your needs, and how you will allocate the funds. Time is a finite twenty-four hours in a day. Workwise, where do you allocate the biggest chunks of time? How much time do you spend on the things you know will amp up your results (not to mention your job satisfaction)? A Time Portfolio grounds us so we can achieve our dreams instead of indulging in fantasies. Tracking how you spend your time enables you to reallocate it for higher fidelity between what you want to accomplish in the bigger picture and what you do every day.

Put It into Practice

I'll use my client Jasmine's Time Portfolio to illustrate the four-step process.

Step One: Identify your categories
Begin by establishing a list of categories where you spend the largest chunks of time during your working hours.

Step Two: List current percentages
Now write down the estimated percentage of time you spend on each bucket. Make this an educated guess; it doesn't have to be completely accurate but does need to add up to no more than 100 percent. Over half my clients total this up to 120 percent—or more! Mistake #1.

Be sure to overlay your time portfolio with a "rhythm of your business" calendar—things that happen annually, quarterly, monthly, weekly, etc. Jasmine's looked like this:

Table 1: Categories and Current Percentages

Category	Current %
My manager's staff and review meetings	15
Managing my team	25
Email and other communication channels	25
Industry socializing and networking	3
Annual events	2
Cyclical business activities	20
Strategic planning and new ideas	10

Step Three: Establish future percentages

Now that you know where you stand, where do you want to get to?

For your next step, list the goal percentage where you'd ultimately like to end up for each category. Record that, going down the list.

This is how Jasmine's took shape:

Table 2: Future Percentage

Category	Current %	Future %
My manager's staff and review meetings	15	15
Managing my team	25	20
Email and other communication channels	25	15
Industry socializing and networking	3	10
Annual events	2	5
Cyclical business activities	20	15
Strategic planning and new ideas	10	20

Now, *hold right there*, because this is where many of my clients make Mistake #2: they expect to shift the percentages from today's numbers to their ideal future number overnight. I know you probably want to nail this right away (I see you, Flash), but it doesn't work that way. Move to Step Four to see how to avoid this mistake.

Step Four: Set intermediate percentages

If your future goal is where you'd ultimately like to be, your intermediate goal is the increment you will set to get you there. Step Four involves choosing a modest increase or decrease in percentages that are *reasonable and immediately attainable*. For each percentage shift, include a corresponding action step.

Here is Jasmine's Time Portfolio including her Step Four:

Table 3: Intermediate Percentage + Actions

Category	Current %	Intermediate %	Future %	Action step
My manager's staff and review meetings	15	15	15	n/a
Managing my team	25	22	20	Reduce one-on-ones from weekly to biweekly
Email and other communication channels	25	22	15	Kill all pop-up notifications and turn off email for one hour a day
Industry socializing and networking	3	5	10	Schedule monthly lunches with a buyer
Annual events	2	5	5	Attend one additional online conference annually
Cyclical business activities	20	17	15	Attend business reviews quarterly instead of monthly (delegate to directs)
Strategic planning and new ideas	10	14	20	Block two hours a week on my calendar for strategic thinking

Choose one or two items that are most important for you to make progress on and deploy your action step. Mistake #3 is to try to shift the percentage allocation of all categories at once. At the end of each month, look back and assess how you did. Not what you *think* you did, but how you honestly did based on your tracking. If you hit your mark 75 percent of the time, you can then increase or decrease, setting the appropriate goal for the next month. For example, if you said you'd spend 20 percent on email and actually spent 40 percent of your time, next month's goal is—you guessed it—to get to 35 percent, not 20 percent.

An interesting thing happens when clients ultimately reach their ideal percentages in the Time Portfolio. With the busyness and minutiae they have been mired in swept away, they're often left with a temporary sense of unease. Remember, all that busyness and other Sole Provider habits served a purpose, feeding whatever hunger drove them. The question now is, what will you replace them with?

After we'd worked together on her Time Portfolio for about six months, Jasmine shared a common reflection with me.

"I've managed to free up my calendar," she said. "But now I'm anxious. If I'm not busy all the time, then I feel like I'm not producing. If my calendar is empty, I'm not needed or wanted . . . like I've lost some power."

"That's wonderful!" I said.

Jasmine looked understandably confused.

"This is a key moment," I explained. "This is what we've been working toward. You've delegated, adopted healthy meeting and calendar practices, and shifted your Time Portfolio so you're not wasting time on old habits. You're now freed up to do exactly what you are uniquely qualified to do."

All the work you've been doing in learning the art of being a good boss has led you to this moment. Take your dedication to leveling up as proof that you absolutely have what it takes to write a powerful new chapter on the freshly emptied slate.

 Time Portfolio Micro Habit

Set an alert for halfway through your day to check if you've spent time on the most important item in your Time Portfolio. If not, what will you shift to switch your attention?

CHAPTER FOURTEEN

Recalibrating When You Lose Your Passion and Purpose

From the time he was a boy growing up in Nairobi, Malik wanted to do big things. In our initial session, he told me about an uncle he'd greatly admired who made a success of himself after Kenya gained independence in 1963. Before his mother's brother built the company that supported his extended family and gave Malik his first job at age fourteen, Malik's family had been among the many impoverished in his country, seven people living in a small one-bedroom house. Now, as a fifty-eight-year-old successful entrepreneur, Malik has never forgotten the gnawing hunger in his belly that kept him awake night after night sleeping head-to-toe with his two brothers on a narrow mattress.

Malik and I began working together about two years after the tech company he built went public. Following in his revered uncle's footsteps, the boy who'd grown up unable to afford medical care, let alone college tuition, had revolutionized education software and lived in a stately home thirty miles north of New York City. Among the first things Malik did when his bank account hit six figures was to establish a mentoring program for teenagers in his hometown. My early sessions with Malik were mainly focused on cleaning up his calendar so he was less bogged down by endless meetings easily fielded by others. Always thoughtful and deliberate in our sessions, about eight months into our working relationship, Malik logged on looking particularly pensive. It did not take much prodding for him to offer what was on his mind.

"I've cleaned up all the mess," he said. "Everything is running smoothly, but it still feels like drudgery. I am so grateful and blessed that I succeeded in what I set out to do. I feel ridiculous saying this, but I'm just going through the motions. There's no joy in this anymore."

Malik had hit a turning point common in many people's stories: he'd lost the plot.

Each one of us has a story. That story is framed by our earliest dreams and current-day status, its plotline moved forward by our individual sense of purpose. In other words, our "why." Why are you striving, why do you want to succeed? Whether the answer is financial security, to take care of your family, change perceptions, reduce your carbon imprint, drive change, make a difference for others, have a powerful voice, or change the world, we all need a reason to get up every day and do the work. That sense of purpose is the driver of our narrative; it pulls us up out of bed and into the fray, sustains us when things get hairy, and inspires us to forge ahead.

Losing the plot is deeply entwined with pressure as both a cause and a cautionary tale. When you lose your sense of purpose and meaning, joy goes along with it, and you quickly land in bewildering *Why am I doing this again?* territory. Without our why, everything is harder. The pressure gets compounded into misery, which leaves us more vulnerable to the further corruption of pressure. What felt challenging before now feels impossible. Disappointments become disasters; what irritated you now triggers an all-out hissy fit. Our guardrails get dangerously worn down, leaving us susceptible to other Power Gaps and Pressure Pitfalls.

As I shared with Malik, losing the narrative can be either the end of our story or an exciting plot twist toward a new one. Thankfully, my own story featured the latter.

As I mentioned earlier, when I reached a certain level of seniority at Microsoft, I became eligible for an eight-week sabbatical. I took it mainly because it was something I'd never done, and I'm drawn to things that scare me. I figured I'd never in my life taken a pause from the relentless push of hard work; let me find out what that would be like. I also figured it would do me some good. I was still young, in my thirties, so it wasn't showing on my face, but I was consistently tired. I didn't realize how drained I was until on my first day of doing nothing a wave of exhaustion hit me with such force as I was driving home from errands that I had to pull over onto a side street and take a nap. True story. I slept for about forty-five minutes in my car. When I awoke, my first thought was *Something is very wrong.* It was ten in the morning.

I went to my doctor, who ran a battery of tests. Turns out I was fine. Physically, that is. For the next few days, I slept upward of eleven hours a night, plus took two or three naps throughout the day. I wasn't depressed—that I knew. I was just exhausted. Adrenaline had been coursing through me so consistently for so many years, my mind was giving my body permission to crash now that I had the time for it.

Over the next couple of weeks, I visited a friend in New York City and started the small theater company I'd always wanted to launch. I also began working with my first coaching client, Gina, at the suggestion of my father-in-law. That still left me with a lot of time to sit on the couch and eat bonbons. I'd never had this kind of Blank Space in which every ounce of brain energy wasn't going toward work, and in that stillness, I had a clear realization. My whole life, I'd been gunning to get to the top, and I was on track to fulfill that goal. It was not a question of if I'd be made a corporate vice president at one of the world's leading tech companies, but when. I'd cracked the code. I knew the formula, I knew the steps needed, and I knew I could get there. *But I didn't want it.* The challenge was gone. Why would I spend the next five years of my life relentlessly chasing something that I didn't want?

It was disorienting. To get to the top of the top had been my personal career ambition for as long as I could remember. Then there was the cultural aspect. I mean, what kind of brown woman who stands to join the elite corporate ranks in America says, "Nah, no thanks"?

At a loss, I called a friend, Laura, and said, "I have no idea what to do next." I considered just cashing out my stock options and leaving, but that thought lasted about half a minute. Laura said, "You seem to like this stuff you're doing with your client. I'm sure Microsoft has a department that does this kind of 'people stuff.' What about that?" There was, indeed, a people development group at my company, but did I really have any business doing that? Just to test the waters, I reached out to the woman who ran that department. Barbara had recently seen me speak at a conference, so I figured it was worth an exploratory discussion. To my shock she said, "I'll hire you right now."

I told Barbara I still wasn't sure. My next stock option vested in a few weeks; maybe it really was time to go. She said, "Come back and I'll hire you for three weeks." My technical friends with whom I discussed this opportunity thought I was crazy. "You can't leave. You're a woman in the tech world, that's a rarity." But Barbara would try me out for three weeks and my current boss would take me back if I wanted, so what did I have to lose?

When I left, I was a group program manager a few years away from becoming a corporate vice president (no brown woman had ever reached that level at Microsoft). When I returned from the sabbatical, I officially moved to HR. I packed up my eyeball collection, and off I went to my new office building across campus. (Yes, you read that right; I used to collect anything related to fake eyeballs. Stress balls in the shape of eyeballs, translucent paperweights with eyeballs in the center, pens with eyeballs on top, eyeball marbles, little clickety-clack walking eyeballs.)

My mandate was to create a training program for 11,500 managers within the company. The demands on the group that ran management training far exceeded what the small team of four people could deliver. To date, only four company-wide classes had been created for managers. I didn't know anything about adult education at that time, but again faced with a scary unknown, I was all in.

When the three weeks were up, I didn't even realize the clock had gone off. Every six months thereafter, Barbara would ask if I was renewing my contract, and it wasn't even a question. My old rush of energy and passion had returned; I had a "why" again. I was buzzing because I was learning new things every day. Before, the products I'd worked on were used by billions, and I got a charge out of seeing people use them on planes and cafés, but I never felt a personal connection. During coaching sessions and workshops, however, I saw the lightbulbs go on in people's eyes as they connected the aha moment with an action they could take. My work was meaningful because I could see the impact right away. I would wake up in the morning excited with ideas, looking forward to whatever work I was doing that day. I finally understood what people meant when they said they were thrilled to be able to do something they would have done for free. As someone who doesn't drink alcohol or do drugs, this was a real high.

Not every lost narrative means you need to quit or radically change your career path. Sometimes, yes, but other times all that's required is a redistribution of your energy and focus. Malik realized that building and creating new education opportunities for those without privileged access was his baseline purpose. In discussion with his board, he brought in a COO to run the day-to-day operations so he could focus on ways to expand the business.

Losing the plot of your life and passion can be surprisingly easy. Everyone wants something from you at every moment, so in that mode, who has time to think about what we want to do versus what we *have* to do?

I use the Joyline tool outlined below with clients to help them escape this peril of feeling drained and miserable and instead spend their days feeling energized and fulfilled.

The Joyline: Rediscover Your Passion and Purpose

At its heart, the Joyline tool is about identifying your sense of purpose and meaning. When we make those internal drivers our North Star, rather than outward goals or to-do lists, we not only feel lighter and happier but have a much greater and more lasting impact.

This is the tool to pull out when:

- You are lacking motivation or finding it hard to concentrate
- You are not getting the same level of gratification from your work as you once did
- You know something is off but are not quite sure what it is
- You are wondering any variation of *Is this all there is?*

Put It into Practice

Step One: Create a list of ten to twenty critical moments in your lifetime up through today. While life is filled with big moments, we're aiming for the highest and lowest points in your trajectory. These moments should include the experiences that most elated you and the pain points that left you despondent.

By way of example, let's look at my client Ella's Joyline. Ella was feeling cranky, burned out, and overall unhappy in her job as a staff writer for a business publication. Here was her rearview mirror list of highs and lows:

Highs

- Meeting my closest friends in high school
- Getting my first article published when I was in college
- Traveling through Europe on my own
- Being promoted in my first job
- Starting an industry networking organization
- Painting the coffee table in my studio apartment
- Taking my daughter on a trip for the first time as a single mother
- Winning a high-profile journalism award

- Meeting my husband
- Getting our dog

Lows

- Being yelled at in first grade by the teacher for something I didn't do
- Having to go to a sports summer camp where I didn't fit in
- When my longtime boyfriend cheated on me
- Bad press episode shortly after I started my business
- Difficult writing project with a problematic client
- My dad's death
- Being diagnosed with breast cancer (and the subsequent surgeries and treatment)

Step Two: Draw a simple vertical line. Then plot your critical points along the line in chronological order, with the high points going on the right of the line and the low points on the left of it. See how Ella's looked on page 230.

Step Three: Identify the recurring themes in your plotted Joyline that form an overarching narrative. To tease out these themes, ask yourself:

- What are the common factors?
- What sensations or feelings underpin the highs as a whole?
- What made all your highs meaningful for you?
- What sensations or feelings underpin the lows as a whole?
- What was it about each of your highs or lows that made such a memorable impression on you?
- What actions did you take (or not take) that show up consistently in either or both categories?
- Who was present/absent in your highs or lows?

PAST

Being yelled at in first grade by the teacher for something I didn't do

Having to go to a sports summer camp where I didn't fit in

Meeting my closest friends in high school

When my longtime boyfriend cheated on me

Getting my first article published when I was in college

Traveling through Europe on my own

Bad press episode shortly after I started my business

Being promoted in my first job

Starting an industry networking organization

Painting the coffee table in my studio apartment

Difficult writing project with a problematic client

Taking my daughter on a trip for the first time as a single mother

Winning a high-profile journalism award

My dad's death

Being diagnosed with breast cancer (and the subsequent surgeries and treatment)

Meeting my husband

Getting our dog

LOWS　　　　　　**PRESENT**　　　　　　**HIGHS**

Here is what took shape for Ella:

High-point themes:
- Having a sense of agency
- Accomplishment
- Belonging
- Genuine connection
- Creativity

Low-point themes:
- Shame
- Not belonging
- Sense of helplessness/being overrun by a situation, person, or an outcome I can't control
- Fear of speaking up for myself

The question is, of course, what to do with this information. You can, if you choose, stop here. Often just seeing one's own themes in a clear light is enough of an aha moment to motivate people to take steps toward realigning with what fulfills them and letting go of what drains them. They see what provides meaning and what takes them off course, what is relevant and what's superfluous. Your Joyline can serve as a conceptual understanding of your purpose and a wake-up call when you've veered off course.

Or you can continue on. It would be great if what you generated enabled you to simply navigate life and work according to your Joyline, incorporating joyful elements and avoiding harmful ones. But as we know, we can't always do what's fun and fulfilling and escape what we dislike. We can, however, identify where our efforts have maximum impact, to determine where to invest our energies and where we need to shore up support.

With your Joyline acting as your compass, you can apply many of the tools you've read about with an intentionality that generates greater personal satisfaction as well as professional impact. For instance:

- **The Delegation Dial** is a tool to know how to delegate effectively; the Joyline acts as its counterpart, informing *what* you delegate. Which tasks on your list energize you and which drain you? What parts of your work speak to your high-point themes? Which are more aligned with your low points, and can those be delegated?

  Sometimes the results of this exercise can surprise you. For years, everyone told my client Dave, the COO for an international corporation, that he should delegate the annual planning of the company holiday party. It ate up the majority of his energy in the fourth quarter of every calendar year, and this was something he could have handed off to his right-hand person. However, after doing the Joyline exercise, Dave identified generating opportunities for cross-community exchange of ideas as a core source of joy for him. He didn't want to delegate planning the annual gathering of executives from around the world because it fed that high-point value. Realizing this enabled him to see the planning of this event as a "get to" rather than another "have to" on his long list of responsibilities. Instead, Dave chose to delegate the planning of the summer picnic that did not feed his Joyline theme in quite the same way.

- **The Time Portfolio** enables you to apportion your time to maximum effect. When you apply Joyline themes to your thinking, you can allocate your time according to what your inner compass is magnetized toward. For instance, let's say tackling new frontiers is a Joyline high point for you. How can you arrange your Time Portfolio to allow for more business development?

  The Joyline themes can also energize the tasks that you can't necessarily cut back on. For instance, let's say genuine connection is a core Joyline value for you, as it was for Ella. If your role demands multiple one-on-one meetings each day, why not spend the first few minutes of each meeting fostering that personal sense of connection with the direct report across from you? For all you Flashes out there who are already *"yeah, but"*-ing the time this will waste, let me assure you it takes no more than 60 to 120 seconds to ask about someone's kids, inquire about their commute in the lousy weather that day, or get their take on a current event. This is far from a waste of time!

- **The Hunger Tracker** helps you identify the underlying wiring that causes you to get activated in certain situations. Many people find they can draw a straight line from their low-point themes to their unmet hungers. This provides a deeper understanding of how and when they may be complicit in the entanglements born of increased power and pressure.

  Ella, for instance, identified not belonging as a low point theme throughout her Joyline. Within minutes of doing this exercise, she connected the dots between her general sense of crankiness and an exhaustive inner need to volunteer for every opportunity so as not to miss out. Seeing our patterns play out with this level of consistency can be both sobering and empowering. As psychology and mindfulness practices teach, this kind of awareness of our patterns allows us to see them clearly and then, from that clear-eyed perspective, make new and better choices.

- When doing the **Cost vs. Benefit Analysis** for any tool throughout, ask yourself, *How can applying this tool align with my Joyline themes? What do I stand to gain that will feed my high-point themes?*

- When using **Mapping** to inform your team how you work best, consider which of your Joyline themes are worth mentioning

so they know what makes you most happy and what drags you down.

As author Adam Grant wrote, "Happiness is not about reaching your goals. It's about aligning your goals with your values." To that I would add: happiness fuels success. If you want to achieve the success you're seeking, understand and align your actions with what makes you feel most alive.

 Joyline Micro Habit

Set a timer to go off once per day to pause and note how you're feeling right in that second. Are you energized and content? Frustrated? Bored? How does the activity you are engaged in connect to your Joyline high or low points? Just like when we see a curve in the road, and we almost automatically adjust the steering wheel to maneuver around it, clients have told me that simply noticing their in-the-moment emotions and connecting them with their Joyline themes has helped them shift their action choices.

PART FIVE

MAINTAIN THE UPWARD TRAJECTORY

CHAPTER FIFTEEN

360 Yourself to Stay on Track

The tools throughout this book will enable you to upgrade your boss skill set as you continue your upward trajectory. And as before, every new level you reach means a new view and new roles . . . and with that, new chances for blind spots to form and your pressure guardrails to get unintentionally worn down. That is why it is so crucial to continue to work the diagnostics and tools to course correct.

As not every one of you will have a coach who can run a 360 process like the one I conduct with my clients to assess where power and pressure have—usually unbeknownst to them—created roadblocks, this diagnostic tool will enable you to self-assess where you might be vulnerable or veering off track.

360 Yourself:
Assess Where You Stand and What Needs Improving

Below you will find a chart containing all the Power Gaps and Pressure Pitfalls covered in Parts Three and Four. For each, I've recapped the array of clues to sleuth out whether that gap or pitfall may apply to you. As you go through, you'll rate each on a scale of one to five according to what's true for you right now, one being "strongly disagree" and five being "strongly agree." The ones you rate a five are the ones requiring your attention.

360 Yourself

For each statement below, highlight your response using a 5-point scale where 1 = strongly disagree, 3 = neutral, and 5 = strongly agree.

#	Question	Strongly disagree	Disagree	Neutral	Agree	Strongly agree
	THE POWER GAPS **The Singular Story**					
1	You feel (or have in the past week felt) defensive or righteous	1	2	3	4	5
2	You've lost curiosity about others' ideas or perspectives	1	2	3	4	5
3	You're met with silence from your team and/or are wondering why no one offers ideas or solutions other than you	1	2	3	4	5
	THE POWER GAPS **Communication Fault Lines** **Uneven Feedback**					
6	You hear rumblings of employees feeling unappreciated	1	2	3	4	5
7	You deliver feedback that is critical more often than positive	1	2	3	4	5
8	You deliver praise (like "good job") without mentioning the impact of the employee's work	1	2	3	4	5
	THE POWER GAPS **Communication Fault Lines** **Assuming Cluelessness**					
9	You don't have your team's full attention when you speak	1	2	3	4	5
10	When delivering critical feedback, you launch in without asking how employees perceive their performance	1	2	3	4	5

#	Question	Strongly disagree	Disagree	Neutral	Agree	Strongly agree
11	When teaching something, you begin at square one without first assessing others' knowledge	1	2	3	4	5
	THE POWER GAPS **Communication Fault Lines** **Sage Speak**					
12	The work product your team is producing does not match your directives	1	2	3	4	5
13	Your team repeatedly asks for clarification of what you mean	1	2	3	4	5
14	You use jargon or insider references	1	2	3	4	5
	THE POWER GAPS **Communication Fault Lines** **Verbal Overkill**					
15	You interrupt others or talk over them to get your point across	1	2	3	4	5
16	You speak the most out of anyone in meetings	1	2	3	4	5
17	You repeat yourself, you repeat yourself, you repeat yourself . . .	1	2	3	4	5
	THE POWER GAPS **Communication Fault Lines** **The Past Experience Divide**					
18	You notice your team members' eyes glazing over as you speak	1	2	3	4	5
19	More than once you've heard someone on your team remark that yes, they've heard that story before	1	2	3	4	5

#	Question	Strongly disagree	Disagree	Neutral	Agree	Strongly agree
THE POWER GAPS **Communication Fault Lines** **Unspoken Messaging**						
20	Your words or expectations are misunderstood	1	2	3	4	5
21	Others infer something about what you think or feel that is not so	1	2	3	4	5
THE POWER GAPS **The Myth of the Exceptional**						
22	You believe you have earned certain leeway given your performance	1	2	3	4	5
23	You let yourself off the hook for bad behavior because you have good intentions	1	2	3	4	5
24	You justify your actions with a *"yeah, but"*	1	2	3	4	5
THE PRESSURE PITFALLS **Unmet Hungers**						
25	You are not getting the results you'd like and don't know why	1	2	3	4	5
26	Your reactions to everyday occurrences are bigger than the situation objectively warrants	1	2	3	4	5
27	You feel slighted, offended, or threatened by a colleague's actions	1	2	3	4	5
28	You believe you need to prove your relevance or importance	1	2	3	4	5
THE PRESSURE PITFALLS **The Sole Provider Trap**						
29	Your team is highly dependent on you for answers and input	1	2	3	4	5

#	Question	Strongly disagree	Disagree	Neutral	Agree	Strongly agree
30	You take on others' work (and have noble stories about why you do so)	1	2	3	4	5
31	Your plate is overloaded	1	2	3	4	5
32	No one offers ideas or solutions other than you	1	2	3	4	5
	THE PRESSURE PITFALLS **Mired in Minutiae**					
33	Your to-do list is consistently long	1	2	3	4	5
34	You have the sensation of not being able to get out from under your giant workload	1	2	3	4	5
35	You have big projects you never seem to be able to get to	1	2	3	4	5
36	You have no time or bandwidth for strategic thinking	1	2	3	4	5
	THE PRESSURE PITFALLS **Superhero Syndrome**					
37	You say yes to every opportunity or request	1	2	3	4	5
38	You are run down physically and/or mentally	1	2	3	4	5
39	You do not make time for self-care	1	2	3	4	5
	THE PRESSURE PITFALLS **Losing the Plot**					
40	You feel unfulfilled or unhappy in your job	1	2	3	4	5
41	You cannot connect to a sense of purpose or meaning in your work	1	2	3	4	5
42	You find yourself wondering any variation of *Is this all there is?*	1	2	3	4	5

Now that you have your very own 360, albeit just done by you on you, tally up the items you've rated as a five. Those are the Power Gaps and Pressure Pitfalls that demand your attention right now. Refer to where each is discussed in previous chapters and create a plan for applying the corresponding tools to steer around and out of those trouble zones.

The trick to long-term success is doing this assessment not just once, but routinely. I recommend revisiting this assessment every six months to check in and see where you are and what areas might need tweaking. Learning is not something we do once and are done. To keep growing, you need to be ruthless in your pursuit of illuminating your blind spots and regulating your emotional responses in the face of pressure. You must continually self-diagnose what might be getting in your way and work the tools with full presence. And then keep going as if your success depends on it.

Because it does.

Conclusion

You picked up this book because you wanted to upgrade your skills as a manager in your work life. And guess what? What you discovered here can also greatly impact your personal life. Managing is a skill set we need to enhance the productivity and well-being of our work teams, but also to enrich our personal lives at home, in our relationships, families, as committee chairs, or in volunteer positions. Many people I've worked with over the years have told me how applying these tools has improved their marriages, created harmony with friends and family, and made their efforts as committee chairs or community members more effective.

Each diagnostic and tool you've read in this book can be applied in myriad ways. Here are a few:

- Use a *"yeah-but"* as an invitation to shift to a *"yes, and."* For instance, *"yeah, but"* your partner repeatedly leaves their dirty socks on the bathroom floor might also be a *"yes, and"* they always make sure my car's registration and inspection are up to date.

- If you're stuck in a Singular Story about a neighbor who gets under your skin, look for multiple meanings to broaden your aperture and consider what else might be true about them other than your absolute perception.

- Feeling tyrannized by your personal to-do list, like you never have enough time to do the things you want to do? Use the Time Portfolio on page 216 to chart how you allocate your nonwork hours and apply the same steps to shift from overwhelmed to empowered.

- If being the only one in your family responsible for making and executing plans feels frustrating, take another scroll through the Sole Provider Power Gap descriptions beginning on page 172 and the 360 Yourself tool on page 237 to diagnose where you may have inadvertently trained them to rely on you rather than themselves.

- When heading up a committee, if you find yourself mired in the minutiae of tasks you are convinced that only you can do right, turn to the Delegation Dial on page 187 to shift some tasks to others in a way that sets you both up to succeed.

- In a funk and not quite sure why? The Joyline tool on page 227 can help you chart your personal high/low matrix to track where you're investing your time and recalibrate toward what brings you joy and passion.

Here comes the best part: the more we upgrade our skill set at work, the more we feel enlightened and empowered outside the workday—and vice versa. We become better bosses, better spouses and partners, better parents, and better community citizens. Our experiences, both professional and personal, are made richer as we see ourselves and the path forward with clarity, inspire others, and make a potent difference in the world around us.

Isn't that, after all, why you wanted to become a boss in the first place?

Acknowledgments

Creation is never a solo sport. As a first-time author, I owe a heavy debt of thanks to many writers, editors, researchers, thought partners, family, and friends.

Over a decade ago, my husband, Matthew, said, "You're sitting on a gold mine of data from your 360 interviews. You ought to write a book." Thank you, Matthew, for planting the seed, and for your continuous and generous support, ideas, feedback, and roll-up-your-sleeves-and-do-whatever-it-takes-to-help-Sabina presence.

A huge thank-you to Debra Goldstein, collaborator extraordinaire. You brought clarity to the page and doggedness to keep us both hammering at a concept until we really *got it*. No matter where my writing journey takes me next, I'll always have your voice in my ear: "If it's not clear on the page, it's not clear in your head."

Thanks to Jen Marshall for expertise on all things book-into-the-world and Laura Nolan, my wonderful agent, for being a fierce advocate, providing a clear vision, and helping translate and untangle the many steps along the way. Laura's ideas, creativity, and clearheaded thinking make her someone I'm lucky to have in my corner. Stephanie Frerich, your belief in my expertise, your ideas, editing, and partnership are things most first-time authors only dream of. Thanks to the amazing team at Simon & Schuster, including Brittany Adames. Thank you to Geraldine Collard from Penguin Random House UK for your thoughtful comments and bringing this book to readers in the UK. Thanks, Suzanne Rothmeyer, for a jaw-dropping eleven-hour photo shoot and the work to prep and follow up, and to the team at Candid Goat—Becky Sue Wehry, Cindy Cowherd, and Kendra Cagle—for a revamp of my website and brand.

Lisa Phelps Dawes has helped me become a better writer, though I don't think I can ever get to her level of witty prose. Thank you, Lisa, for jumping in with encouragement, discouragement (when I had a stupid idea), and being a model *"yes, and"*–er. Your skill and professionalism have helped me take my work, including all the work that goes into bringing a book into the world, to the next level.

Thank you to my editor at *Harvard Business Review*, Courtney Cashman, for multiple conversations providing input on early ideas as the concept for this book took shape. Marcia Zina Mager helped me surmount the deeply personal demons of fear and doom that prevented me from getting started. Erin Brenner, Maris, and Amy Jameson assisted in the early days of formulating a proposal. Sarah Drumm did a lot of heavy lifting putting together research and materials for the book proposal, helped me with countless 360 reports, and much, much more. Your professionalism and quality of work is something I treasure. Kathleen Kenney analyzed thousands of pages of verbatims to validate the themes across interviews. Heather Hunt has helped with dozens of interview reports, scores of brainstorming sessions, reviews of the proposal, and portions of the book. Above all, she has become a friend who drops everything to help me out whenever I need her wisdom and expertise. In addition to your many gifts as an editor, the biggest gift you've bestowed on me is your trust. Many thanks to David Moldawer for your sharp writing and keen sense to home in on the core message as I worked on the final version of the book proposal. Thank you, Elana Brief, Tim Dawes, and Graham Bullen. Your contributions made this book much better and allowed me to see it through readers' eyes.

I'm deeply grateful to my parents, Jehanara Nawaz and Huzur Nawaz, who provided me with an exceptional education and opportunities. My sons Zaref and Ziven have been truth-tellers, ensuring I always check the mirror they hold up before I go out in public. My parents-in-law, Jim and Audrey Anderson, are endlessly curious about my latest work; thank you for your support, love, and ideas.

My late brother, Ahmad Nawaz, and late brother-in-law, Eric Anderson, inspired me by publishing their books and encouraging me to write my own. My late friend, Edree Allen Agbro, spent many evenings helping me ideate and keeping me company by phone during long commutes. Not related by blood but equally close to my heart, I will always remember Jalil—a man who lived in our building and helped with chores while extending unfailing faith in my ability to succeed no matter the challenges I was facing, and Egbert Bhatty, who read and commented on every article I wrote and had blind confidence not just in my ability to write a book but certainty it would be a great one. If any of you were still here, I hope you'd say I've done you proud.

Thank you, Andrew Feldmar, for your wisdom, love, support, and teaching me to stand up for myself as queen of my own queendom.

One of the many ways in which my life overflows with abundance is friends who encourage me with words, acts of generosity, and support. There are too many to name, but you know who you are. I am especially grateful for support from the following people in the process of my writing journey: Thank you, Arianna Dagnino, Asli Aker, Beth Kahn, Carla Forester, Caron McLane, Elana Brief, Gillian Donavan, Graham Bullen, Jane Gregg, Jill Hufnagel, Karen Parrish, Kelleen Wiseman, Kristen Lane, Lisa Phelps Dawes, Michele Ng, Molly Carr, Ruchira Dasgupta, Sanjukta Pal, Suze Woolf, Tim Dawes, and Valerie Galvin.

As numerous as friends are the authors and thought leaders who chose to encourage me, mentor me, and champion my work. Thank you, Whitney Johnson, for goading me to write this book—for years—and thanks to Dorie Clark, Rita Gunther McGrath, Kim Scott, Arianna Huffington, Peter Block, Barry Oshry, and Kevin Kruse.

This book is about bosses, and I'd be remiss not to mention my good fortune to have had so many great ones: Nathan Williams, Bob McBreen, Blake Irving, Tom Reeve, Mike Mathieu, Barbara Grant, and Liz Welch. Thank you also to the people who trusted me as their manager and worked on the teams I managed.

Lastly, a big thank-you to my clients. Your courage to show up every day and make tough decisions, face criticism, seek feedback through the 360 process, persist, play big, and grow your teams leaves me in awe. I owe so much to your trust, open dialog, and the stories and ideas in this book. I have learned from and am inspired by each of you. Thank you also to everyone I interviewed for feedback on my clients—your willingness to share thoughts (especially the critical feedback) allowed my clients and me to do our work.

Sources

Chapter One: New Level, New Rules

What Got You Here Won't Get You There: How Successful People Become More Successful, by Marshall Goldsmith (Hachette Books, 2007)

Redefining Success

https://hbswk.hbs.edu/item/the-best-ceos-share-the-spotlight-with
-their-teams

https://www.mckinsey.com/capabilities/people-and-organizational
-performance/our-insights/givers-take-all-the-hidden-dimension
-of-corporate-culture

https://link.springer.com/article/10.1007/s10551-022-05228-5

Understanding Hidden Power Dynamics

The Practice of Adaptive Leadership: Tools and Tactics for Changing Your Organization and the World, by Ronald A. Heifetz, Marty Linsky, and Alexander Grashow (Harvard Business Press, 2009)

Adjusting to the Spotlight

If I Understood You, Would I Have This Look on My Face? My Adventures in the Art and Science of Communicating, by Alan Alda (Random House, 2017)

Chapter Two: Common Boss Myths and Mistakes

Satya Nadella

https://news.microsoft.com/source/features/innovation/empathy
-innovation-accessibility/#:~:text=%E2%80%9CMy%20per
sonal%20philosophy%20and%20my,something%20Rene%20
Brandel%20experienced%20firsthand

Empathy

https://www.catalyst.org/reports/empathy-work-strategy-crisis

"yeah, but":

https://www.pwc.com/ee/et/publications/pub/sb87_17208_Are
_CEOs_Less_Ethical_Than_in_the_Past.pdf

Authenticity

The Five Invitations: Discovering What Death Can Teach Us About Living Fully, by Frank Ostaseski (Flatiron Books, 2017)

Act Like a Leader, Think Like a Leader, by Herminia Ibarra (Harvard Business Review Press, 2015)

https://ozanvarol.com/the-downside-of-grit/

Chapter Three: The Obscuring Effect of Power

Storycraft: How to Teach Narrative Writing, by Martin Griffin and Jon Mayhew (Crown House Pub Ltd., 2019)

Chapter Four: The Hidden Impact of Pressure

Amygdala hijack

https://news.illinois.edu/view/6367/670955, https://www.forbes.com
/sites/tracybrower/2021/09/19/empathy-is-the-most-important
-leadership-skill-according-to-research/?sh=318b8f3f3dc5

Emotional Intelligence: Why It Can Matter More Than IQ, by Daniel
Goleman (Bantam, 2006)

https://onlinelibrary.wiley.com/doi/abs/10.1002/job.2289

https://www.linkedin.com/pulse/costs-amygdala-hijacked-leaders
-jens-hartmann-ph-d-dozent/

Chapter Five: The Foundational Tools

Cost vs. Benefit Analysis

"Change or Die," by Alan Deutschman, *Fast Company*, May 1, 2005.
https://www.fastcompany.com/52717/change-or-die

https://charlesduhigg.com/how-habits-work/

*Immunity to Change: How to Overcome It and Unlock the Potential in
Yourself and the Organization*, by Robert Kegan and Lisa Laskow
Lahey (Harvard Business Press, 2009)

*The Practice of Adaptive Leadership: Tools and Tactics for Changing
Your Organization and the World*, by Ronald A. Heifetz, Marty
Linsky, and Alexander Grashow (Harvard Business Press, 2009)

Micro Habits

https://health.clevelandclinic.org/why-people-diet-lose-weight-and
-gain-it-all-back

https://ideas.ted.com/heres-how-i-finally-got-myself-to-start-exer
cising/

*The 5 Second Rule: Transform Your Life, Work, and Confidence with
Everyday Courage*, by Mel Robbins (Savio Republic, 2017)

https://community.thriveglobal.com/microsteps-big-idea-too-small
-to-fail-healthy-habits-willpower/

The Yes List
https://www.apa.org/news/press/releases/2015/10/progress-goals
https://www.huffpost.com/entry/the-power-of-writing-down_b_12002348
Zen Mind, Beginner's Mind: Informal Talks on Zen Meditation and Practice, by Shunryu Suzuki (Shambhala, 2006)
The No Asshole Rule: Building a Civilized Workplace and Surviving One That Isn't, by Robert I. Sutton (Business Plus, 2007)

Chapter Seven: Identify Your Communication Fault Lines

Uneven Feedback
https://www.gottman.com/blog/the-magic-relationship-ratio-according-science/
https://zengerfolkman.com/articles/the-vital-role-of-positive-feedback-as-a-leadership-strength/
https://www.fastcompany.com/90724596/this-is-what-happens-to-your-brain-when-you-give-and-receive-compliments

Assuming Cluelessness
Shame vs. Guilt—Brené Brown (brenebrown.com)
https://onlinelibrary.wiley.com/doi/abs/10.1002/job.2553
https://www.ncbi.nlm.nih.gov/pmc/articles/PMC8526793/
https://www.researchgate.net/publication/363296145_Shame_Does_It_Fit_in_the_Workplace_Examining_Supervisor_Negative_Feedback_Effect_on_Task_Performance

Shut-Up Muscle
https://www.psychologytoday.com/us/blog/play-your-way-sane/202108/were-worse-listening-we-realize

https://www.ncbi.nlm.nih.gov/pmc/articles/PMC7075496/ (multitasking)
https://marshallgoldsmith.com/articles/adding-too-much-value/

Sage Speak:
Made to Stick: Why Some Ideas Survive and Others Die, by Chip Heath
and Dan Heath (Random House, 2007)
https://www.journals.uchicago.edu/doi/abs/10.1086/261651 (curse of
knowledge)

Past Experience Divide
https://www.forbes.com/sites/carolinecenizalevine/2021/06/23/new
-survey-shows-the-business-benefit-of-feeling-heard--5-ways
-to-build-inclusive-teams/?sh=6be967ec5f0c
*The Empathy Effect: 7 Neuroscience-Based Keys for Transforming the
Way We Live, Love, Work, and Connect Across Differences*, by
Helen Reiss, MD (SoundsTrue, 2018)

Chapter Eight: Dispel the Myth of the Exceptional
https://hbr.org/2019/04/the-psychology-behind-unethical-behavior

Solicit Feedback
https://focus.kornferry.com/the-organisational-x-factor-learning-agility/

Part Four (intro)

Effects of cortisol and stress
https://emeraldpsychiatry.com/is-there-a-connection-between-stress
-hormones-and-thinking-ability/#:~:text=The%20Brain%2C%20
Cortisol%20&%20Stress:,not%20fully%20backed%20by%20data.
https://www.ncbi.nlm.nih.gov/pmc/articles/PMC5619133/

Working memory tools
https://www.ncbi.nlm.nih.gov/pmc/articles/PMC6596227/#:~:text
=We%20demonstrate%20that%20goal%2Ddirected,neural%20
substrate%20of%20fear%20learning
https://www.ncbi.nlm.nih.gov/pmc/articles/PMC4207727/

Deep breathing
https://resbiotic.com/a/blog/breath-and-mind-hrv-amygdala-and
-how-to-improve-your-mental-states

Grounding exercise
Mindfulness : The 5-4-3-2-1 method by Dr Ellen Hendricksen (mastic
-lifestyle.com)

Chapter Ten: Root Out Unmet Hungers

*The Origins of You: How Breaking Family Patterns Can Liberate the
Way We Live and Love,* by Vienna Pharaon (G. P. Putnam's Sons,
2023)
*Immunity to Change: How to Overcome It and Unlock the Potential in
Yourself and the Organization,* by Robert Kegan and Lisa Laskow
Lahey (Harvard Business Press, 2009)

Chapter Eleven: Steer Clear of the Sole Provider Trap

Caretaker
https://karpmandramatriangle.com/

The Flash
*Managing at the Speed of Change: How Resilient Managers Succeed and
Prosper Where Others Fail,* by Daryl R. Connor (Random House,
1993)

Chapter Twelve: Get Unstuck from the Minutiae Web

Blank Space

https://www.scientificamerican.com/article/mental-downtime/

https://www.huffpost.com/entry/silence-brain-benefits_n_56d83967
e4b0000de4037004

https://www.researchgate.net/publication/259110014_Is_silence
_golden_Effects_of_auditory_stimuli_and_their_absence_on
_adult_hippocampal_neurogenesis

"The Making of the Corporate Athlete," by Jim Loehr and Tony
Schwartz, *Harvard Business Review*, January 2001

Chapter Fourteen:
Recalibrating When You Lose Your Passion and Purpose

Joyline

https://www.threads.net/@adamgrant/post/C17Ska6rGpM

About the Author

Sabina Nawaz is an elite executive coach who advises C-level executives and teams at Fortune 500 corporations, government agencies, nonprofits, and academic institutions around the world. As a speaker and coach in high demand, Sabina delivers dozens of keynotes at professional conferences each year and teaches faculty at Northeastern University and Drexel University. During her fourteen-year tenure at Microsoft, Sabina worked in software development before changing tracks to lead the company's executive development and succession planning efforts, advising Bill Gates and Steve Ballmer directly. She has written for and been featured in *Harvard Business Review, The Wall Street Journal, Forbes, Inc., Fast Company*, NBC, Nasdaq, and *MarketWatch*.